YES

YOU CAN

IT ALL STARTS WITH YOU!

Written By: *Vivian Risi*
with Susy Alexandre

Tellwell Talent
www.tellwell.ca

ISBN
978-0-2288-1157-2 (Hardcover)
978-0-2288-1156-5 (Paperback)
978-0-2288-1158-9 (eBook)

TABLE OF CONTENTS

HOW IT ALL STARTED . . .

Twenty-three minutes can feel like a lifetime. With 10,000 eyes staring up at me in excitement and anticipation of the speaker they had all been waiting for, I could hear the loud beating of my heart as I wondered, *Vivian, what are you doing here?*

I recall a few moments prior to that, as I walked up the steps backstage, preparing myself for the biggest introduction of my life. Turning back to where my kids stood and meeting their eyes, my daughter, clearly sensing my nerves, gave me a reassuring look and said, "Just breathe slowly, Mom."

Breathe. Right. It seems like a thing that might be hard to forget, but at the time, it was exactly what I needed to hear. I inhaled deeply and found my breath. Man, was it bright out there! I peered out at the audience. It was all so surreal!

Earlier that day, I had spent some time bonding with the MC, James Cunningham. I shared with him an idea I'd had for my walk onto the stage. I wanted to be able to calm my nerves and, at the same time, prevent myself from tripping up and falling on my face. I figured, if I danced my way over to the microphone and happened to stumble, the music and the energy of the moment would make my misstep less noticeable. So, I asked him if he could dance along with me to "Happy" by Pharrell Williams. He smiled, high-fived me and roared, "I love that song!" I figured this strategy would not only calm my nerves, but also give me a chance to get in sync with the beat of the crowd, setting the tone before I started speaking.

I made it to the podium and looked out at the sea of people in front of me, all of their excited faces looking back. I peered down at my notes . . . this had been so much easier with the music blaring. *Ok*, I thought to myself, *just breathe and read the notes you've been given. You're about to introduce the great Tony Robbins!*

I just needed to read through my lines, and everything would be ok. I made it three quarters of the way down the page when someone slipped a piece of paper on top of my notes! *What just happened?* Glancing to my left, I realized the MC was standing beside me, gesturing down at the paper that was now blocking my notes. My heart skipped a beat as I read the words scrawled onto the small sheet:

SORRY! TONY'S NOT HERE. HE'S STUCK IN TRAFFIC!

Oh, okay. Tony's stuck in traffic.

Wait—WHAT?! Tony's WHAT?! Stuck in traffic???

My mind started racing. *What am I going to do?* I couldn't help but think, *this must be my fault somehow—I must have done something wrong. I need to get out of here! Someone please just pull the fire alarm and SAVE ME!*

I could sense the mounting anticipation of the crowd, and I knew I had to do something—anything—to keep the ball rolling. Seeing as my notes didn't cover the man of the hour being stuck in traffic, I was going to have to figure this one out on the spot. I took a deep breath and smiled out at the audience, hoping to convey confidence while racking my brain for my next steps. I hadn't planned on being on stage for more than a few moments . . . But what is it they say? The show must go on! There was nothing to do but work with what was available to me in the moment. So, on a whim, the MC and I started to engage in some off-script banter, going back and forth as though it were all part of the show. We played off the energy of the crowd and, miraculously, everything seemed to flow from there.

We were in the zone as we chatted about business and life, and I shared with the audience how it is that I came to be at my first Tony Robbins show over 20 years ago. The audience was into it; they wanted to hear more! Feeling my comfort level rise, I was connecting with the room—feeling as though these people could really relate to what I was saying. Being on stage speaking to countless strangers wasn't second nature but passing on my experiences and sharing my lessons with others just *felt* right.

That day was one for the books as I faced yet another fear and found myself completely at ease—all while completely outside of my comfort zone—speaking in front of thousands of people.

I remember the moment Tony finally arrived. As I went into my introduction, his video started up on the screens behind me, and the lights dimmed. It was then that Tony walked over to me, larger than life, shook my hand and said, "Great intro, Vivian."

That day had such an impact on me and, apparently, on others as well. Soon after the event, I began to receive emails and phone calls from people who wanted to know more about my story, people who wanted to know who I was. The event organizer had asked if I would be open to sharing my contact information with any attendees that might want to get in touch after the show. Of course, I was happy to do so, but I never expected the response that I got! I was floored—and completely flattered—to hear that my words had resonated with so many people.

If there was one thing I hoped might come out of my experience that day, it was that I might be able to help someone, even just a single person in the crowd. I wanted to be able to give someone the same spark of hope in their journey that Tony had given to me when I had attended his show for the first time.

Soon after that day, I received an email that stood out from the rest. It was from a publisher in the city. He said he had heard me speak and was intrigued by my story, asking if I would I like to meet to hear his thoughts. *Sure*, I thought, *why not?* We met at a small coffee shop in the city, and he went on to tell me a bit about who he was and why he believed I should be writing a book. I guess it shouldn't have come as a shock that this was what he wanted to discuss but upon hearing the words, I thought to myself, *Me? Write a book?* The same person who spent her high school years being told not to bother with university? The same person who never managed to fit into the mold? How could it be that someone believed I should write a book? I'm not a writer, and even though I love books, I rarely have the time to read them. I'm an audiotape listener for crying out loud!

I took some time to consider his offer. By our second meeting, I found myself warming up to the idea. By our third meeting, we were seated at the round table in my office, with my children present, passing papers back and forth between us as I signed on the dotted line. I may not be a writer, but that didn't mean I didn't have a story to tell. My instincts were speaking up, and I knew deep down that this new project was meant to be a part of the next chapter of my life.

Like everything else on my journey, the concept and creation of this book were anything but smooth sailing. Knowing I would need the help of a writer in getting my thoughts out onto paper, I did my best to connect with the writers assigned to me—yes, you read that right—*writers*, as in, more than one. But without that necessary connection, that real joining of minds, it just wasn't working.

Ultimately, I would have to seek out my own writer and go to battle on my vision before the pages of this book could be written. Everyone on board had good intentions, but I needed to be absolutely clear about what it is I wanted for this book, and what it is I *didn't*—which I quickly discovered, is easier said than written.

Then there was the matter of determining what genre the book would fit into. This was far from easy! How do you define your journey? How do you take your life's lessons and decide where on the shelf they belong? Business? Biography? Self-help? I couldn't choose. To be honest, my life has been anything but neat or pre-packaged, and the last thing I wanted for this book was to force it into a mold that God knows I never fit into myself.

So, we got to work on *just writing*. We figured we would let the book speak for itself and leave it to you, the reader, to decide where on your shelf it belongs. While I may not be able to tell you EXACTLY what the book is (I'm hoping it will be something very unique to each person who reads it) I can tell you what it isn't. This book is not an autobiography. Not in the traditional sense, anyways. When narrowing down what would make the cut, I had zero desire to relive every detail of my life chronologically in these pages from baby to boardroom. You can also rest assured I won't be lecturing you about the formal etiquette of business practice or attempt to counsel you on every aspect of the corporate climb. And I'm certainly not a doctor, so if you're looking for statistics or a simple prescription for success, you won't find it here.

Think of these pages, instead, as the greatest hits of my journey so far—from good to bad to life altering. These are the moments in time and lessons of my life that have afforded me the hard-earned wisdom that I now look to share with you. I'm no exception to the rule, and that's the point. Just like Tony stood on that stage and inspired me with his honesty and humility, it's my greatest wish that this book, and the lessons within it, might connect with you in some similar way. By sharing my personal experiences and guiding principles, I hope these pages serve to inspire and illuminate you to the limitless potential of your own life.

For me, the most important feature of this book was that it be honest. I began this project with the primary goal of connecting with others, and I truly believe the philosophies

I've shared go beyond any industry or demographic. This is, quite simply, an honest collection of life lessons from someone who knows the benefit in passing it forward. Read this book cover to cover, or skip ahead to whatever strikes you most, and when you're done, I hope you find yourself inspired to add the next chapter to your own story.

CHAPTER ONE

IT STARTS WITH YOU

*The people who get on in this world are the people
who get up and look for the circumstances they want,
and if they cannot find them, they make them.*
—George Bernard Shaw

Let me begin by telling you one thing I know for sure: *it all
starts with you.*

You can't expect to be of value to anyone else—in business,
or otherwise—until you discover and embrace the immeasurable, untapped value within yourself. This recognition
and understanding of who you are at the core will play a
vital role in your personal development and journey toward
living your best life. Whether you seek fame and fortune, a
healthy and happy relationship, or simply a sense of fulfillment and satisfaction with your personal accomplishments
at the end of each day, your best life is waiting, and it's
everything you envision it to be.

Whatever it is you're after, it has to start with you. This is
a philosophy I've held to for as long as I can remember, the
idea that if good things were going to happen in my life, it

was going to be up to me. I alone would have to decide what my future would look like, and I would have to be the one to go out and chart the course.

When it comes to living your ultimate life, you may struggle with what that really means. What is your "ultimate life" anyway? I believe it has to do with redefining this idea of success, tapping into what that word means to *you* and how it plays into your overall vision for the future. Success doesn't have to relate solely to your work life or your finances; in fact, your definition of personal success should go above and beyond all of that!

Think of your ultimate life as a blueprint by your own design, uniquely crafted by your own journey and pursuits. Keep in mind, most people won't envision ultimate success in the same way—to each of us it means something infinitely different. Some of us may see ourselves at the top of a podium, a gold medallion around our necks, the crowd cheering our name—the hard-earned payoff for a champion. Others envision those closest to us seated around the dinner table, a unit with roots that will continue to grow on long after we take our leave—a family. There are those of us who picture the corner office, that shiny brass plate on the door, the title we answered to for so long now ours, a glittering footnote that follows a comma every time we sign our name—someone else to now fetch the coffee and sort our calendar.

There's no right or wrong way to envision your dreams— that's why they are, after all, *your* dreams. Picture them as big and bold or as small and sweet as you want, but never do yourself the injustice of leaving them on the shelf to collect dust. Do everything in your power to turn these dreams into reality; do absolutely everything and anything possible to realize them.

Your first step? Working from within!

YOU are the catalyst for your greatest life—it all starts with you. Let me say that again—IT ALL STARTS WITH YOU! Say that out loud every morning if you have to, from the moment you wake up and open your eyes. Every day is another opportunity to make your dreams happen. Do whatever you need to, but just *do something*—ANYTHING! The life that you dream of isn't going to unfold at your feet by chance; it sure as hell didn't for me.

My family came to this country in 1958 with little means and even less of a grasp on the English language. We were immigrants in every sense of the word—alien to this place and the people in it. The daily struggles for my parents were simple: steady work and food on the table. It was survival mode as we stumbled about, learning to navigate our way in this strange new world.

I was a pre-teen in 1967 when adolescent tragedy struck in the form of acne. My smooth skin was now covered in painful red bumps; ones that I knew could stay with me as scars, marring what had so recently been a clear complexion. This was a small problem in the grand scheme of things, I realize now, but tell that to a 12-year-old girl who's trying desperately to fit in amidst a sea of peers whose looks, speech and lives are nothing like her own. Did I really also need to be the girl with what looked like chicken pox scattered across her face?

At the time, there was no "search" button at my disposal. There was no Google to give me answers and point me in the right direction, and even if there had been, can you imagine trying to explain the concept of Internet to two people who still balked at 8-track tapes? I shudder at the thought . . . No, going to my parents was simply not an option. For one thing, having a sister whose face remained unblemished already had my parents under the assumption that my acne problem was somehow self-inflicted—maybe something I ate, they would suggest, or some new soap I'd used? It was clear that this issue was one I would have to resolve on my own.

So, I pulled out the phone book and got to work, eventually coming across a contact for a dermatologist in the city. I pooled my loose change, mapped out a bus route and made my way to the appointment. Once there, the physician explained to me that what I needed was a combination of treatment by sunlamp and a medication called Tetracycline—both of which would cost money I didn't have. I was a 12-year-old girl looking for the cure to pre-pubescent acne. Suffice it to say, at this point in time, no one expected much from me, or my pursuit of unblemished skin. But here's the thing: I expected more from me. Giving up was never a thought. I saw a problem and started taking the steps toward what I hoped would be a solution. I was moving from A to B to C with the hope that some combination of trial and error would eventually land me where I wanted to be—in this case, acne free.

Around this time, my older sister was working at a snack bar at a local strip mall. There was a small popcorn stand that formed part of the snack bar, and it was there that I saw my chance to make the money I needed to treat my acne. Through my sister, I was able to set up an interview with the manager.

Mary Purvis was a strong woman, the "take no guff" kind. As she looked me over, I was relieved to see a small but kind smile break the tension in her face. Was she impressed—or amused? In that moment, I wasn't sure. I was just 12 years old, and in spite of my tall stature, there was no doubt Mary wasn't about to be fooled into thinking I was of legal age to work. I readied myself for the rejection, but instead she hastily pulled some forms from a shelf as she told me, "We're going to make you—oh, we'll say 16—and we'll need to get you a social insurance number, too." I couldn't believe it! *Hurray*, I thought, *I just got my first job!*

Mary was instrumental in my first foray into the workforce, and I can still hear her voice as she would instruct me, sergeant-style, of the proper way to butter toast in the snack bar. "When you butter the toast, you SLAP IT ON," she would say, as she would smack a dollop of butter onto the crispy bread, "and SCRAPE IT OFF!" A frugal woman, she knew the value of a dollar, and it was her keen business sense and strong leadership style that was never lost on me. I worked every shift I could get, alternating between the popcorn stand and snack bar. I was making 95 cents an hour, and with all the shiftwork I had taken on, it wasn't long before I could buy the sunlamp and medication the dermatologist had prescribed.

I wish I could tell you that these two things in combination immediately cleared up my skin, but that wasn't the case. After nearly burning my face off, and doing more harm than good, I eventually figured out (via some very painful trial and error) how to properly use the sunlamp and medication to its purpose. As a side note, I do not recommend burning your skin under a heat lamp to resolve acne concerns. Fortunately for acne-sufferers today, this is no longer the prescribed method.

At the end of the day, no one is immune to struggles, and they really do come in all forms. From big to small, you're going to find that at one point or another, this life will hit you from all sides. Try not to take it personally. It's in these moments that you can either get moving toward a solution or roll over and admit defeat. That sunlamp might have burnt out the first day, or I may have never gotten the job I needed to pay for it, but by taking those first steps toward a different outcome than the one I was headed for, I was validating my own self-worth—and in effect, investing in myself. I was worth working toward the outcome I desired, and that was reason enough to get up and do something about it.

There's no investment more worthwhile than your own happiness. But coming to grips with who you are, and what it is you want, will always come at the cost of experience—some good, some less so.

After securing my first job just a year earlier, I found myself, at 13, ready for a new challenge. One evening, my older sister came home donning a sparkly crown and sash. She'd just won top prize in a citywide beauty pageant. It would be a short-lived victory, as she was about to get married and therefore be ineligible to go on to the finals for the title of Miss Italia Canada . . . But that didn't mean there wasn't still someone in the family interested in competing!

Despite being three years under the minimum age of entry, I submitted myself as a contestant for an upcoming pageant, another qualifier for the finals in Miss Italia Canada. Trying to look as "grown-up" as possible on the day of, I caked on the makeup and took out my ponytail, letting down my long hair. When it was my turn, I smiled and attempted to walk gracefully across the stage. On the outside, I tried to look calm and confident. On the inside, I was a ball of nerves, wondering just what the heck I'd gotten myself into! I have to admit, once my nerves began to subside a little, the whole thing was a thrill! It was a new experience, something different from my everyday routine. I was taking a risk and putting myself out there—and it felt really good.

Before I knew it, the evening was coming to a close and the winners were being called out over the cheering crowd. When they called my name, I could hardly believe it—I'd won first place! I had only entered the pageant on a whim, craving a new experience and looking to challenge myself. I hadn't even considered what would come next if I won, and now I was on my way to the next stage—Miss Italia Canada! I was so excited, but also terrified. The pageant would be held in Queen's Park—an event on a much bigger scale than the one I had just experienced. How would I pull this off a second time?

My family rallied together for the finals, and given the focus on the Italian community, I could feel the pride from my parents as they looked on from the crowd. So, there I was, playing dress-up in my big sister's clothing, standing under the scorching spotlights, at just 13 years old. I looked around at the other contestants: all beautiful, mature young women considerably older than me, and all more qualified than me to take the crown. I remember thinking, *Oh my*

God, what am I doing here? What happens if by some miracle I win? What if they find out about my age? What if . . .?

This whole thing had been a challenge for me from the start; I had jumped headfirst into something I (a) didn't meet the qualifications for and (b) had zero experience in. But, so what? It was a challenge, something new I had set out to try, and I'd done that . . . and loved it! Whatever came from the next pageant—I could handle it. It was with that attitude that I held my head up and made my way onto the stage in my big sister's clothes. I may not have walked off with the title, but as I look back now, I still smile as I think to myself: *I had a lot of nerve!*

Competing in that pageant had nothing to do with vanity. It was about the challenge—breaking from the routine of my life and trying something new. I saw the age limit and instead of feeling deterred, I was intrigued. I never set out to win; I only set out to *try*. It was something to do, something fun outside of my usual routine. What did I have to lose by trying?

Just prior to the finals, I was riding high on having won the local community pageant when I was hit with a reality check at the hands of someone who should have been bolstering my confidence. Mr. Stevens was both the principal of my school and the guidance counsellor, so, as far as authority figures went, he was one of the biggest in my life at that time. As I'd been raised to understand it, when someone in a position of authority spoke, you listened. That was all there was to it. Unfortunately, as I sat across from him during a one-on-one meeting for students about to enter high school, I felt anything but inspired by what he had to say. You could say we got off to a poor start as he ushered me into his office, and I told him, excitedly, "Guess what, Mr. Stevens? I won top place in a pageant!" To which he smirked and replied sarcastically, "Must have been the Miss Congeniality prize."

It was at that meeting, as I neared graduation and approached high school, that, acting as my guidance counsellor, Mr. Stevens advised me not to worry too much about my studies going forward.

"Don't bother," he told me, "you'll never make it to university." He went on to say that I would likely soon be more focused on the roles of wife and mother, anyway—titles which, in his opinion, were no doubt in my near future. He did, however, advise that I take Home Economics . . . Gee, thanks. Needless to say, I was devastated!

While I believe that Mr. Stevens' uninspiring "words of wisdom" were probably the same ones given to every other girl in my grade, I can't help but wonder if his delivery was especially harsh in my case. There was just something about me that rubbed him the wrong way. In a sea of students willing to fit the mold, he saw me as a rebel. And without realizing it, or ever intending to be rebellious, I guess I sort of was. I had grown up with an independent spirit, and that had always set me apart. I suppose for myself, even then, the idea that "one size fits all" just didn't work for me.

In spite of this, Mr. Stevens' words did not fall on deaf ears; the effects of that meeting stayed with me for a long time. His views of how my life would unfold and the roles he felt I was destined to play weren't new to me but hearing them out loud from someone in his position made a very real impact on me. I was someone who, up to that point, always felt beyond my years, was always eager to break down barriers and at the very least, *try*. But it was moments like these, feeling so dispirited by the opinions of someone I was told to respect, that had me wavering in my convictions.

Who was I to think I knew better than an adult, an authority figure—someone in power? I felt defeated and resigned to a fate that had been laid out for me without my consent. It was around this time that I began to really feel the pressures of an internal battle brewing; one that had me struggling to juggle who I truly was with who I was expected to be. Still, my penchant for going against the grain would carry on as the learning lessons and opportunities of my life continued to reveal themselves in unexpected ways . . .

When I was 16 years old, I worked part time behind the counter at a health club in the city. My role was simple: greet members, handle the sign-in—the basics. My official title was *Instructress*, as it read on my badge—no name, just *Instructress*.

I enjoyed my job. I found myself in my element as I developed a rapport with members, suggesting classes that might be better aligned with their specific goals and in effect, adding value to their experience. I wanted to help clients in getting the results they were after and making the most of their time. The company philosophy was centered on bringing in new members, but *my* aim was all about giving existing gym-goers added value to their experience. Before long, members were letting management know just how much they enjoyed the personalized service they got with me.

Almost immediately, the higher-ups took notice. Registration numbers were up, and clients were raving about "that Instructress girl, Vivian." And then one day, my manager, Muriel, approached me with big news. Dave Wakefield—the president of the company—would be making a trip down from the US-based headquarters to meet the girl credited with their recent spike in re-signs.

Wait—the president of the company was flying down to meet *me*? I couldn't wrap my head around it.

Dave Wakefield was less of what you might imagine a typical business owner to look like and more reminiscent of one of those hardcore-bodybuilder types. He was tall, handsome and clearly a fitness fanatic. Of all the scenarios I had played out in my head prior to meeting him, none compared with the brevity and impact of the real thing. In true "boss" fashion, he walked up to me, asked me a few short questions and then shook my hand firmly before saying, "You remind me of me." I still remember how it felt to get that compliment—that short but satisfying affirmation that my efforts were both acknowledged and appreciated. There wasn't much more to it than that, but a short time later, I was promoted to the role of assistant manager.

This had been an early glimpse into business leadership for me. When Dave Wakefield had learned of an employee making strides to grow the business, he took it upon himself to personally come down and put a face to a name. I would never forget the positive effect this had on me, and in the future, I would strive to apply this to my own leadership practices. At present, this feeling is one I try to pass on to members of my team at every opportunity, always reminding them that their contributions are not only recognized but also vital to our success.

My promotion wasn't all good news. I now had to contend with my co-workers—many of whom had been rattled by this sudden dissension in the ranks and now felt justified in giving me a hard time. They hadn't expected the young, bubbly part-timer to do more than sign people in and smile; who was I to think I could do more? Who did I think I was?

It was an early lesson in the double-edged sword of achievement as I discovered just how lonely it could be at the "top." This is a big issue for many people—the idea that stepping outside of your comfort zone and doing the unexpected might be met with the alienation of your peers—the consequences of falling out of step with the crowd. One thing I've learned from moments like this one in particular is that personal achievement is often two-pronged. There will always be a give and take to everything you do, especially when you break apart from the status quo and rise above expectations.

Is it worth it? Absolutely. No question. YES.

I hadn't expected anything to come from my efforts at the club; I was just doing what came naturally. Looking beyond what was expected was a natural instinct of mine, always aiming to do more and go further. In the case of the fitness club, I had done more in my role than I was supposed to and was recognized for it—and that put a few peoples' noses out of joint. At the time, I couldn't understand why, but eventually I figured it out.

Not everyone is banking on your success, and it's an unfortunate reality that you should anticipate the naysayers along with the cheerleaders. People will often feel threatened and unnerved by those who break from the herd and disrupt the system. Don't let it stop you! You can't control the reactions of others, and not everyone is going to be cheering you on at every step of the way. Stay focused and present, always harnessing positivity to keep you motivated—especially in moments when others may try to dampen your spirits.

When you invest within, you see beyond the limits set in place, and you equip yourself with the confidence to do more—and in effect, *be more*. Respect yourself enough to see YOU as the ultimate investment and learn to shake off the haters. Barriers in life will vary—there will *always* be something or someone that stands between you and your goals. Anticipate it. Accept it. Learn to cope and look beyond. If you find you can't see beyond the obstacles in place, *imagine* something better and get to work on creating that new reality. Maximize your efforts in everything you do, and always aim to surpass expectations.

No one can exercise control over your self-worth unless you grant them that power. Get into the habit of reflecting on your positives, as well as working diligently to improve yourself where needed. It's all about evolving as you make these strides toward your ultimate life. First you start from within, and then—and only then—can you aim to take on the world.

When I sought to go beyond my job description at the fitness club, I did so without realizing it. In my mind, I rationalized, *If I'm investing my time here and the gym is investing in me as an employee, I'm going to do the best I can and be present in the moment.*

Any space or situation where you've elected to dedicate time and energy is an opportunity. It's a chance to either grow and learn or stay exactly as you are. Everything about growth is a positive, because when you're moving, there's always that next step and those endless possibilities around the corner.

Albert Einstein defined insanity as doing the same thing over and over and expecting a different result. If you're unhappy with the status quo, but you continue to do the same thing over and over, never stepping outside of yourself or testing the limits, nothing will ever change. To grow and live your purpose, you must be willing to work from within and get outside of your comfort zone. Those first steps toward change are the hardest, so if you've been looking for a sign, I'm here to tell you . . .

Get off that hamster wheel and GO FOR IT!

Do something. Anything. Just break routine and see what happens!

It's never too late to start working on yourself and chasing your goals. Some people find their groove early on in life, while others get on track much later. When it comes to living out your authentic life, the only clock you're on is your own. Make the most of your time and find a pace that works for you.

I once read about a woman from England who was aboard a delayed train on her way to work and began to dream up an idea for a story. So inspired by what she'd imagined, the woman embarked on a near decade-long journey towards crafting and sharing that story with the world. All the while, she faced the grief and pressures that follow family death, birth, divorce, and immense financial struggle. Still, she persevered and turned her idea for a story into the outline for a series of books that would go on to become some of the best-selling books in history.

J.K. Rowling is the woman behind *Harry Potter*, and while she's notoriously tight-lipped about her exact net worth, her fortune has been estimated in the hundreds of millions, with some reports even placing her closer to the billions. Not bad for a woman who was living on welfare well into her thirties. From a daydream on a train to success beyond measure—it's the journey in between that makes the difference, and it all starts with you.

CHAPTER TWO

BE PREPARED TO TAKE RISKS

In a world that is changing really quickly, the only strategy that is guaranteed to fail is not taking risks.
—**Mark Zuckerberg**

Nothing good ever comes easy. Throughout my journey, I've often been faced with situations that had me feeling like every move I was making was the wrong one, where every risk just seemed to dig me in deeper. I would wonder, *Am I doomed?*

The answer, of course, is no, I wasn't doomed. But, boy oh boy, did it ever feel like it! Over time, it wasn't so much that my circumstances changed; rather, it was a shift in my attitude. In learning to translate the opportunities around me differently, I was able to look at things like "risk" from a new perspective.

I've discovered that the idea of risk is all about perception. It's in our nature to see risk as a negative. Everything about the word brews up feelings of uncertainty. This is a result of years of adverse associations being drilled into our minds. From a very early age, we are told we should always steer *away* from situations involving risk. However, dealing with risk doesn't always have to mean something bad is going to happen. Instead, you can re-program your way of thinking to look at situations in a more positive and constructive way.

What is risk, anyway? I like to think of it as something rooted in potential, where undetermined losses and gains may stand in the balance, but where a learning opportunity is always certain. I believe another reason we fear risk is because it means working with unknown variables and taking chances that may be calculated to some degree but hold no guarantees. Funnily enough, it's these unknown variables and "risky" opportunities that have formed such a large part of my professional—and personal—growth.

In the early '90s, I was working as an office manager for a brokerage, living in a tiny apartment as a single mother with my three growing teens. In that year alone, we'd had to move three times. Trying to keep up my children's morale, not to mention my own, was getting harder every day. It was the lack of stability in my home life that had me the most motivated for change.

Around that time, I had already taken my first steps towards what I hoped would be a more certain future for my three kids. I had signed on as an office manager knowing it would afford me a steady income and structured work hours. I had given up my right to sales commissions and life as a successful agent, but I was putting my family first. I was making the moves necessary to give my children the secure and nurturing home life I envisioned for them. I now had a schedule that would mean more time for my children, and that was top priority. Sure, I was making less money, but I now had a steady paycheque coming in, allowing me to better juggle my roles and put my focus where I felt it was needed the most—at home. For my children's sake, I was more than happy to put the title of "superstar realtor" on the backburner. My children were supportive, and I loved my office.

I thrived in this newfound stability for about four months. That's when the rug got pulled out from under me. The corporately owned brokerage had been sold to a large American company that had announced the sale of all their locations. With no one in line to buy my office, I knew what that would mean for me. So I rolled up my sleeves and got to work.

As the potential impact of what this might mean for our office began to set in, I kept focused and did my best to ignore the rumors being thrown around by my competitors. There was buzz that the office would be shut down, while others predicted it might be serviced from one of the purchasing company's larger local offices. Everyone seemed eager to prove they had the inside track on what would come next. But while *they* speculated on what was in store for us, I worked on a plan to save my job.

I called everyone I thought might be interested in buying our small, 18-agent office. I had a list of names in mind—people who I knew could benefit from purchasing this office, and who could continue to grow it—so I got them on the other end of the line and did my best to explain why this opportunity was tailor-made for them. I think back on my efforts; trying to express to each person down the list just what value lay ahead for them in purchasing the business, just what they stood to gain—while I stood to lose it all. I treated each call as if it were the only one on my list, determined to find my buyer.

Instead of letting myself spiral out, I had gone into recovery mode. My instincts had kicked in as I held an encouraging and supportive front for my people. In spite of my competitors' efforts to recruit those on my team by spreading rumours and inciting panic, I approached our situation from the other extreme. I spoke about our predicament as the greatest thing that could have ever happened for our office, even suggesting that I wouldn't be surprised if we found ourselves at the centre of a bidding war.

In spite of the "ambulance chasers" at my heels—the competitors hell-bent on taking advantage of our position—I stepped up as a leader and worked to reassure my agents and staff that a new owner was exactly what we needed. A new leader on deck would ensure our growth, I explained, someone to nurture our thriving business. I let them know it was business as usual and to "let me worry about the rest." It was my job to step up and find a qualified buyer, not to panic my team and send our business into a tailspin.

I'd made my way through all but one name on my list, and as I dialed that last number, I considered everything riding on this call. From the moment the broker picked up, I went into sales mode. It didn't take much stretching of the facts because, in truth, this *was* a great opportunity for the right buyer, and I hoped this last broker would see the value in what I was pitching. At the end of my spiel, there was a long pause. I'd anticipated every response *except* the one I got, as the broker on the other end of the line asked me: "Vivian, if it's such a great opportunity—why don't *you* buy it?"

Pause. Me?

Well for one, I thought, *Buy it with what money?* Secondly, and most importantly, the plan had been to be home for my kids, to get a paycheque, to have some stability! In going back to my basic instincts, I was a like a lion looking to take care of my cubs—it was *primal*, and it was priority one. They were at that vulnerable age where they needed guidance the most. My children were dealing with a lot; their parents had divorced, and their home life was lacking the kind of stability I knew they needed. My job as an office manager had been my way of seeing them through these years, and even though the pay had been a quarter of what I was making as a successful realtor, I knew no amount of money could substitute my *being there*. My top concern was my kids. Now that everything I'd been working toward was at risk, all I could hope for was a qualified buyer to step up and keep things as they were.

Unfortunately for me, and as it happens, my plans had unraveled and there was no buyer waiting in the wings to step in and make it all better. I was about to undergo a crash course in adapting to unforeseen circumstances—not to mention, the invaluable lesson in stepping up with a plan B when plan A falls apart at the seams.

There was only one option available to me: I phoned the new president and introduced myself. Rather than putting all my cards on the table, I approached this phone call from another angle, casually implying I *might* be interested in buying the brokerage myself. The last thing I wanted was to come across as too aggressive or eager—this was a negotiation, after all. It occurred to me that my experience in this industry up to that point had readied me for this moment in many ways. I knew all about negotiations, and I was no stranger to adding value to my side of the table. With that in mind, I felt my inner confidence kick in: *You can do this*, I told myself.

I knew I needed to take control of the conversation and steer it to my benefit, so I explained that while, yes, I might be interested, the opportunity had come up unexpectedly, and so naturally, my capital was "all tied up." I went on to suggest that a deal could be made, but there would be terms they would have to be comfortable with, ensuring the financials could be worked out in a way that would be realistic to my situation.

I treated it like any other deal, discussing the details as though we were setting terms on the sale of a home. In working from my background in sales, I leveraged the conversation to make myself of value to them. I was confident in what I could bring to the table, and that came through in my pitch, even alluding to the fact that my buying the office would act as an olive branch in working with the other offices involved. I believed in myself, and I believed in the business. It didn't take much finessing to express what was the honest truth; we both stood to gain here. I could have been intimidated going into this call, but instead I thought back to the nerve of my teenage self, walking across that pageant stage in front of all those people. If I had that kind of nerve then, I could definitely muster some up now. After all, if there *had* been any truth to my former guidance counsellor's words, it was probably that I had the whole "congeniality" thing going for me!

I got every kind of feedback you might expect at the time. People told me that a male-dominated industry like ours simply wouldn't stand for a female lead; they questioned who would even work for me. You could say I had some doubts of my own—I didn't even have my broker's license at this time! But I had come this far, and I wasn't about to let a little skepticism derail me. I took some time to myself to go over all the nagging doubts in my mind, everything I felt I didn't know, all the tools I wasn't sure I had, and then I broke it down further with a checklist. It was important to me to keep focused and getting these immediate issues down on paper would help me work through them constructively—taking it step by step—as I'd always done.

One of the most urgent points on my list was my broker's license. I immediately enrolled for my courses and had someone else step in for eight months as the broker on record. Every problem has a solution, and once I broke it down it was all just common sense.

You don't have a license? Sign up for the courses you need and get one.

Need someone to hold the post while you do it? Get someone! MAKE IT WORK!!

That's what I did.

I signed up for the courses to get my Brokers license, and I worked my ass off, barricading myself in the bedroom of our tiny apartment, studying on the floor into all hours of the night. It wasn't easy—it never is—but I got it done.

The most important item on the list was hiring the right people for my team. There were only so many things I could take on myself before I would be micromanaging and doing more harm than good, so I sought out people who specialized in the areas that I didn't. Once I began to pair my problems with solutions, I was able to focus my energy on the bigger picture and play to my strengths, which has always been dealing with people. In my first year as the broker to our office, we grew from 18 agents to 40. I had leveraged myself against every barrier and found a way to make it work. It may not have been easy, but it was necessary, and because I believed in what I was doing, it was possible.

Ultimately, I took a risk that came with no guarantees and a heavy serving of harsh criticism. But I'd done the math—and despite everything that worked against my favour at the time, I was the only one who could work the situation to my advantage—it *had* to be me. I bought the brokerage and got aggressive about building our brand, armed with no real capital but an excess in drive.

There were always going to be factors outside of my control. For example, the fear of the market dropping was never far from my mind, but these were things I would just have to deal with. These were the moments where I turned to myself and chose to work from within. I understood that my best defense against the unknown would be a solid team. So, that's where I started, and everything got moving from there.

When I bought my brokerage, I didn't have the luxury of time to really think through every facet of the risk I was taking, but in considering my options, I knew the buck stopped with me. If I was the only hope of saving my job, how could there be any other way? Sure, it could have all gone wrong, and I could have ended up back at square one—but at least I'd know that I tried.

When it comes to business, risks are a necessary component of success. Even so, these risks must first be weighed with great measure, and calculated to within an inch of reason. This may seem counterintuitive to the very idea of risk, but when there's something at stake—and there almost always is—it is up to you to do your due diligence first, and leap after. My situation may not have afforded me the time to give this risk as much thought as I would have liked, but I was also coming from a place of experience; having spent so many years in the industry, I knew I wouldn't be stepping into this new role completely blind.

You might wonder, "But what if I'm wrong? What if my risk yields no reward?" Well, if we're being honest—and I think the only way this works is if we are—some of your risks are going to leave you empty-handed. They're going to leave you down and out, contemplating where you went wrong. That's just the nature of the beast—yes, even the risks you think through. Just because something doesn't pan out the way you'd hoped, doesn't mean there isn't still value to be found in the lessons you learn in the process. Your life is going to be spent on the journey, not just the destination, and it's there that you will collect your greatest lessons and most valuable insights.

You have to be realistic; even armed with a positive attitude and a well-thought-out plan, not everything you do is going to be met with immediate success. So, what? Learn from the mistakes and keep trying! Consider your stumbles as life's way of ensuring you come out the other side with your humility intact.

When trying to re-work how your brain internalizes the idea of risk, it can help to keep some potential benefits at the forefront of your mind. After all, if you can anticipate some light at the end of the tunnel, it's that much easier to take those first few steps.

Here are some of the potential gains I call to mind whenever I'm faced with a situation that requires risk:

1) Developing new skills (and fine-tuning existing ones)
2) Overcoming fear of failure and working beyond self-imposed limits
3) Financial gains
4) Discovering hidden opportunities
5) Establishing a higher comfort level with the unknown

DEVELOPING NEW SKILLS

Risks come in all shapes and sizes and present themselves in all manners of situations. Most often, you'll find they arrive in the moments you're feeling the least prepared and even less enthusiastic about tackling them head-on. The very idea of a risk implies some form of negativity or danger. Yet, this often proves to be an excellent opportunity to develop new skills. Where we might otherwise become stagnant in our abilities, the idea of risk means having to discard routine methods and get our brain thinking in new ways. Often, it's these unexpected scenarios that turn out to be just the encouragement we didn't know we needed—also known as a swift kick in the ass—pushing us to develop the skills necessary to manage these "risky" situations to our benefit.

I think back to that first phone call with the new president of the company. I had to pull out every sales tactic in my arsenal, and dabble in some new ones, to sell him on the value I could bring to the table. It was a lesson in dealing with risk and opportunity head-on, and I'm every inch the better businessperson for it.

OVERCOMING FEAR OF FAILURE & WORKING BEYOND SELF-IMPOSED LIMITS

In business, fear of failure can be a killer. It will hinder your self-confidence and prevent you from making the moves necessary to advance your career. Overcoming these self-limiting feelings of doubt and insecurity are vital to your growth—in business and life in general. Even with my back against the wall, and no one in my corner, I had to meet this new challenge head-on, confident and focused. Easier said than done? Absolutely. But it's a must. So, seek out what scares you and stare it in the eye. Often, our fears are so much less than the monsters we've worked them up to be in our minds. If you want to rule your kingdom, you need to slay the dragon that exists in your mind.

Let's put it into perspective: What are you really afraid of? Failing? Landing flat on your face? The judgment of your peers? Missed opportunities?

Well, guess what? These are all the consequences of doing nothing anyway! If you're not even trying—you're failing. If you never fall flat on your face, how will you ever develop the sense of empathy required to relate to the countless others who have? If you look to the validation of your peers for every step you make, you'll never succeed in anyone's eyes, much less your own. If the idea of a lost opportunity haunts you, consider the losses you take every minute you stay sitting there on the bench, refusing to get in the game for fear of the very things that, yes, *might* happen out there, but are *guaranteed* to happen to you where you are.

I've felt that immobilizing sense of fear countless times. I guess you could say it's expected when you're laying the groundwork for your future, but it's *necessary* to move past it, grow from it and push forward.

FINANCIAL GAINS

Let's talk about risk as it relates to the potential for financial gain. Financial gain doesn't necessarily have to come as a direct result of the risk in question. It can also come as a payoff for having demonstrated your abilities in leadership through your initiative in risk management during a critical time. These moments are crucial to your credibility as a member of your team, demonstrating to the people around you—peers, superiors, etc.—that you are willing to bite the bullet for the greater good and act in a way that represents the very best of your brand. These telling moments can often result in promotions, greater responsibility in your role, or the attention of those in a position to seek you out for other lucrative opportunities.

Above all else, these moments tell you a great deal about who you really are.

I think it's fair to say that most businesses, at their core, are essentially a numbers game. As it relates to the idea of risk, I like to break it down to the basics with the following equation:

AMBITION + ACTION = FINANCIAL
SATISFACTION

It doesn't hurt that it rhymes! The reality is there's no shortage of ambitious people in the world who carry with them an immense passion for their cause; but like anything else, it's all just white noise unless it's followed by real action. Taking action—ANY action—is going to work to help you get from where you are to where you want to be. You simply can't go wrong when you're in motion, and when you combine your ambition with the follow-through of ongoing and specific actions, the rewards will come.

While we're on the subject, I should warn you—a fixation on your bottom line is never a good idea when pursuing your goals. Obviously, finances play a very big part of our lives. You can't deny that the almighty dollar makes the world go 'round—but does it do you any favours to design your life around currency? I would never suggest that you turn a blind eye to profit and expect to live on sunshine and smiles alone; this isn't a Beatles song, and it takes real money to stay afloat in this world. What I'm hoping is that as you go forward, you'll begin to see financial gain as more of a happy consequence to living your purpose, in place of it representing the purpose itself. Personal satisfaction, both in work and beyond, must come from a deeper place than our pockets. There must be something of more substance that drives you—or you'll come up short every time.

DISCOVERING HIDDEN OPPORTUNITIES

We've already touched on the idea that some of the truly great moments can be found in the most unexpected of places. When it comes to opportunities, the same potential can be found behind every risk that comes your way. Begin to look at risk as it truly is—an uncertain "thing"—that is, something you can't quite define but that has presented itself on your path. The element of uncertainty is unnerving, but if you don't *really* know what this risk might hold, or what lies beyond it, what basis do you have for assuming it's negative?

I try to view risk as an opportunity in disguise, the potential for adventure, and the possibility of something new I might never have otherwise considered. I took a risk in buying the brokerage in 1993, and while I won't deny it felt anything but thrilling at the start, it turned out to be one of the greatest adventures of my life. Had I not been faced with no other option but to take that risk, I might never have found the courage—or have again been presented with the opportunity—to break the barriers set in my own mind and take the steps toward securing my future.

If you asked me before it happened, if I'd like a glitch in my plans, I would have said no. But there was no room for my input when life's design unfolded all around me, and for that I'm thankful, because it's that sudden risk that stopped me from getting in my own way.

If you look up the definition of risk, it's not pretty. Webster had little inspiration to give when they wrote that one up. So, let's redefine risk by looking at it from a new angle. Instead, when you think of risk, program yourself to immediately replace that word with this one instead: *adventure.*

Google defines *adventure* as: "to engage in hazardous and exciting activity, especially the exploration of unknown territory."

Now THAT'S a definition I can get behind! Skip right over that "hazardous" bit and have a look at those key words:

- ENGAGE
- EXCITING
- EXPLORATION
- UNKNOWN

Get EXCITED about your life! ENGAGE fully in everything that comes your way and stay active in your resolve and in the pursuit of your goals. EXPLORE UNKNOWN territory and pave your own way!

ESTABLISHING A HIGHER COMFORT LEVEL WITH THE UNKNOWN

The greatest opportunities of your life will come unannounced, and there's as much blessing as burden to be had in this. Accept that you can't always control what comes your way but take comfort in the knowledge that you can control how you react and, in effect, everything that comes after.

Nothing good comes easy. Say it with me:

NOTHING GOOD COMES EASY!

Growth and progress involve risk; there's no way around it. You're going to stumble and fall, but it will only help you to better prepare for the next round. Risk is going to come at you fast and hard. It's up to you to be your own center at the eye of the storm, so be prepared to pay attention and reset your sails!

When you start moving forward, the world is going to throw opportunities at your feet, and it's going to be left to you to read between the lines and do the rest. Get comfortable with being uncomfortable because growth is an awkward process; it's not supposed to feel like a day at the spa. You need to develop strategies for dealing with the unknown, methods of breaking down your thoughts and meeting problems with constructive ideas and solutions. Situations involving risk are going to give you lots to think about and leave you with decisions you will need to be make.

When risk has me weighing out my options, I like to recite the facts, both in my mind and on paper, breaking them down to the bare essentials. I've always been in the habit of list-making as a tool to supplement many of the decisions I make on a daily basis—big and small. I often find that if I get the facts out in front of me, there's little room left over for doubt.

Make no mistake, I trust my gut implicitly—I just won't act on impulse. It takes a fine-tuned balance of intuition and due diligence to make an intelligent, calculated risk or decision. To most, this is a vital tool in their arsenal, a priceless skill. Personally, it cost me $1,000,000 for this sense of enlightenment, but we'll come back to that later!

There was a young waitress in the '70s who was working in a little bakery in California. Having finally achieved her goal of completing her college degree and overcoming her struggles with a speech impediment that had haunted her since childhood, she began to dream of opening her own restaurant. But with no money of her own, and none that her parents could afford to give her, she struggled with how to make this dream a reality.

One day, after having vented her frustrations to a long-time patron of the bakery, she was floored when the man returned to her with a loan of $50,000 in cheques and personal commitments from himself and several other customers who believed in her and wanted to lend their support. It came with a note that encouraged her to follow her dreams, giving her 10 years to pay back the loan with no interest.

The waitress was overcome by their generosity. The man who had presented her with the loan advised her that the money should be put into a money market account with a major investment firm—a concept that had been completely foreign to her up until that point. Unfortunately, her assigned broker would mismanage the investment, and after just three months, every dollar she'd invested was lost. Still, the experience was anything but fruitless for the ambitious waitress, as she took the opportunity to learn everything she could about the financial sector. She read every article she could find, taping articles up on her walls and studying figures until they made sense. She had set out to understand what had happened to her money, and along the way, discovered the potential for herself in the financial industry. Shedding her restaurant ambitions, she set a new goal in place: to become a successful stockbroker.

The uphill journey would prove worth it, as she would eventually right the wrongs of her fumbled investment, pay back the generosity of those who had supported her from the start, and build an empire beyond anything she'd ever dreamed.

Suze Orman is an author, financial advisor, motivational speaker and television host with a net worth estimated in the tens of millions. On her success, Orman has noted that had it not been for her initial loss of the $50,000, she would probably still be a waitress today. She credits the experience as the catalyst for the motivation and opportunity that would come after.

CHAPTER THREE

BE A VISIONARY—GROW INTO YOUR GREATNESS

The visionary starts with a clean sheet of paper, and re-imagines the world.
—Malcolm Gladwell

Being a visionary isn't a birthright—it's a choice. You can either choose to grow into your greatness and pave your own way, or you can choose to follow the herd. Sheep or shepherd, it's your call.

I guess you could say I never really played to my pre-defined role in this world. I would say it started from birth. In an Italian family that had already met the quota on daughters—my older sister was six years old at the time—being born a girl when everyone had been hoping for a boy would be my first act of rebellion. I'm sure my parents would deny now what was undoubtedly their disappointment at the time. Though it's hard not to see the fourteen hours of labour—without epidural, no less—that my mother endured with me as a testament to the fact that, to the very end, both my parents had hoped I would change my mind and emerge as a boy.

But that just wasn't in the cards. My story was always destined to be my own and, seemingly, always one that would go against the odds.

The notion of purpose is a fickle one in society today. Many people will try to define you from the get-go, influence what you think you know about yourself, and categorize you in ways that make *them* feel more comfortable. The titles they give you, the names they may call you, and the roles you are told will suit you are all meaningless. None of it means anything unless YOU believe in it.

Growing up in an Italian family of immigrants was not easy by any measure. I was just three years old when we arrived in Canada and settled into our suburban neighborhood, where I quickly learned just how unwelcome I would be amongst my peers. My siblings and I were picked on constantly, getting called names that we had never even heard before, partly a credit to our poor English, I'm sure, but it was a safe bet that the taunts were most likely *not* flattering. What could I do? No one expected any pushback from me, a lanky girl who towered awkwardly over my peers. I was expected to just grin, take it and do my best to blend in. Funnily enough, this would be a recurring theme in societal expectation that would follow me well into adulthood. The pangs of a childhood where I just never quite fit in would be the scars that would ultimately prepare me for a life of standing out and apart from the crowd.

I remember taking the school bus home with my younger brother in tow when I was eight years old. There was a bully (isn't there always?) by the name of Reggie. He was four years older than me and eight years older than his target of the day, my little brother. Of all the bullying we endured during this time, of all the bullies that come to mind, Reggie stands out amongst the rest. He was bigger than most of the other kids his age, and I'll never forget the way he kept a pack of Rothman's cigarettes rolled up in his sleeve. I remember this vividly because I had a clear view of it as I sat, pinned to the seat by Reggie, the smell of smoke and sour on his breath—the consequence for stepping in to defend my kid brother.

What could I do? Apologize? Sit there and take whatever might come next? But then what about my little brother—what would happen to him next?

With my arms pinned down beside me, my head was the only thing left mobile. So, I used what I had and jerked my head to the left, biting down on the fleshy part of his arm just below that rolled up sleeve. I chomped down with every ounce of fear and frustration I had inside, and then I bit down a little harder than that. It would be the last time he ever messed with us, as I learned that Reggie could feel things too.

I still can't believe I did that! I remember that moment, my heart palpitating right out of my chest—it was like something took over, as though every bit of my being just went into survival mode. My instincts brought out this strength in me, this willingness to stand up for myself that I hadn't even realized I had, and I guess it's safe to say it took Reggie by surprise too! It was as though, in that moment, I could tap into this inner instinct of mine to fight the bully.

Keep in mind, beyond the schoolyard, bullies will still appear in all forms. They may be bigger than you or appear stronger. They may represent some kind of authority figure or come equipped with better resources—but none of this matters if you hold on to your faith in your own inner strength.

As a child, your tolerance for the limits imposed on you by others is much lower. If someone tells you what's what, you're quick to disagree. If an authority figure says no, you look for another angle to get what you're after. If someone tells you "no girls allowed"—you start your own damn clubhouse. Children just seem to have this inner confidence, this inherent drive to grow into their authentic selves at any cost. As we grow older, the world around us starts to take shape and we discover that breaking from the norm is no longer viewed as sweet or creative in the eyes of others. This looming pressure to conform hovers overhead, in line with some generic flow chart of who fits where and does what.

Consider this: If you put an empty cardboard box in front of an adult and ask what he or she sees, the answers will often reflect some version of the obvious. But take that same box and put it in front of a child and suddenly the sky's the limit:

"It's a boat!"

"It's a space ship!"

"A racecar!"

This is called vision, and these children are what you might call young visionaries. So, what happened to the rest of us?

What caused us to lose sight of our visionary spirit, as we got older? It's hard to say, but somewhere along the way we stopped looking at the world through our own eyes and started wearing the prescription lenses prescribed by others.

To me, a visionary is someone driven by purpose, someone who sees beyond what's in front of them and is determined to make a difference, to leave his or her mark. Some people believe that visionaries are born with the ability to think outside the box, that these special few have been genetically blessed with the kind of internal wiring that just gives way to greatness. I don't buy it. Visionaries are praised for their innovative ways of thinking, their unique ability to look at something from every angle—all of which can be self-taught. So, let's first begin by talking about the power of innovative thought.

Despite what you may have heard, innovative thinking has not been reserved exclusively for the born-visionary types. To master this skill, all you need is a little practice. It's that simple.

Your brain is currently programmed toward a fairly routine train of thought. You internalize and process things in a way that is familiar to you and, ultimately, arrive at results that fall in line with an overall consistent line of thinking. In other words—you're completely normal!

What we're trying to do is understand how someone can go from an ordinary thought process to one that mimics how a visionary thinks—someone with an extraordinary thought process. This is another one of those times you're going to have to go outside your comfort zone to get some answers.

To change up your way of thinking and open the doors for more innovative ideas, you have to change up your scenery—in some ways, quite literally. Routine only enables the same thoughts and ideas day in and day out, but once you start introducing new elements to your day to day—be it with new places, new people, etc.—suddenly you've freshened up your mental stock and forced yourself to look at old things with new perspectives.

When I first started in real estate, there was no Internet available to me. There were no cell phones to be had, and Google wasn't a household word. Realtors were the first and last word in the real estate game. We were the Internet of the times for our industry.

Brokerages kept their agents in the know by supplying them with daily tear sheets, detailing new listings on the market. The trouble was, by the time these tear sheets made it to our desks, the listings were two days old. I did the math, and 48 hours was just too long to leave a listing open for the competition.

To compensate for this, I quickly got into the habit of getting out the door a little earlier in the morning and switching up my routes to work, ensuring I covered as much ground as possible on my way in and on my way home. By doing something as simple as mixing up my route, I could keep my eyes peeled for fresh listings and maintain a pulse on the area. After all, if there's any adage that rings true, it's the one about the early bird getting the worm.

There was such an advantage to getting the first line on a new listing, I couldn't just sit around and wait for it to fall onto my desk. I had to think creatively to come up with a way to stay ahead of the pack, and it paid off! This small shift in my daily routine kept me on top of the surrounding market, and I was able to get the inside track on new business—a big payoff for such a small adjustment to my routine!

Every day is an opportunity to do something different—so wake up tomorrow and SHAKE THINGS UP!

Start small if you have to but break from your routine in ways that are going to help position you for greatness. You can't just wait for the opportunities to come to you—you've got to put yourself in gear and go after them!

Brainstorming is another method for training your mind to think in fresh and innovative ways. For as long as I can remember, I've always looked at the world as a work in progress—a blank canvas that just needed a splash of colour here, a slight adjustment there. To me, everything could be improved upon. In school, I quickly earned the moniker "daydreamer," spending so much of my time in the classroom with my head in the clouds, even dreaming up ways to re-design the bland space around me. It became a habit of mine to look at something and then re-work it in my own head, brainstorming ways in which it could be better, or just more aesthetically pleasing. I was able to see things not just as they were, but also as they *could* be.

At my first corporate manager's meeting, working at the brokerage that, unbeknownst to me, I would soon buy, I was confused by what I was hearing. What shocked me was that, based on the discussions, there was zero consideration for the challenges the agents faced. It was just about the numbers. If the numbers were coming down, it became a blame game with no one bothering to consider agent support or areas in which to re-invest. Their philosophy didn't seem to include empowering their existing core at all.

I tried to absorb what was going on around me. Having come from the other side of things, I knew firsthand just what obstacles agents encountered in the business and I couldn't understand why upper management wouldn't give it any consideration.

These meetings were focused on the *take*, not what they could put *into* their businesses, and from there I was determined not to follow their lead. I had a vision for change, and I felt inspired to expand on those plans using a different kind of leadership strategy. I thought to myself, *This isn't how I want to manage—I need to do it differently.*

I was committed to creating a place where my agents would feel encouraged to give their input at every turn, where everyone at every level would look forward to coming to work. My vision was to build a team based on a foundation of respect, transparency and an open dialogue.

I plowed forward with these ideals in mind, knowing that my methods would initially be met with skepticism from the other managers. A new approach rooted in re-investment was seen as naïve for the otherwise cutthroat real estate industry—an approach, no less, spearheaded by a female manager! I stuck to my guns and brainstormed further how to create an environment that would support my agents and arm them with the tools they needed to help us in laying the foundation for our future growth.

In the end, that effort to look beyond the status quo went a long way in ensuring success in my role, not just for that period, but also for the long haul thereafter. Keep in mind, only four short months after that, my company would be sold, and face being shut down or moved. Unsettling as the situation was, it gave me peace of mind to know that so many of my agents were supportive in going forward with me after I bought the office. Had it not been for my efforts at creating an environment that made these agents feel respected and heard, this might not have been the case, and I might have been faced with even more resistance in my transition from manager to owner. Always consider the long game and act accordingly—you never know what the future will bring!

As it relates to my team, we get together to brainstorm as a group constantly. We put our heads together to consider what our neighbors in the South are doing, what's happening in similar industries, what kind of market conditions they might be dealing with in relation to ours. We examine the ever-changing resources available to clients and how they might be handling changing conditions. By taking in multiple perspectives, but keeping to a focused dialogue, I can gather valuable input from my agents, which in turn provides me with even more access to innovative streams of thought for our business. Keeping an open mind to the ideas and opinions of others is an invaluable strategy for growth.

You must accept that your ideas and contributions will not always be met with enthusiasm and praise. Sometimes, it will seem that others are not as open to new opportunities as you are, and you can only push so much before you find yourself force-feeding your vision down the reluctant throats of others. In these instances, don't give up—instead, re-work your approach.

Sometimes, your ability to see the bigger picture will mean change, and this will result in resistance from those who feel uncomfortable with the idea of a shift in the status quo. When this happens, hold fast to your resolve and begin to deconstruct your idea into smaller actions or strategies that can be more easily realized. Once others see the results of small victories you have contributed to, they will become more willing to consider your overall vision. The idea is to never break but be willing to bend and be flexible in working with others toward what should ultimately be common goals. Finding ways to see your vision through while still respecting the opinions of others is crucial to your success and credibility as both a leader and member of the team.

It was the '70s and I was in my mid-teens working part time at a women's fitness centre, called Figure Magic. If the name wasn't enough to mark a sign of the times, our uniforms consisted of purple leotards with high heels. This was the same gym that would later reward my efforts with a promotion passed down from the president of the company himself. A little before the accolades and my new title, I worked part time after school and on weekends at the front desk.

From the start, I believed in this company. Fitness centres exclusively for women were a new concept, and this gym had found its place catering to that niche. The money was coming in, and they were opening new franchises steadily across the board. Still, I had some concerns. Our business model seemed wholly focused on new membership sales; capturing new clients was top priority, but there didn't seem to be any emphasis or strategy toward customer retention. One major issue that struck me was the fact that none of our centres offered shower facilities.

What kind of a gym encourages you to work up a sweat but then gives you no option to wash off afterward?

Surely, I couldn't be the only one who found this to be a problem? As a part-time employee in her teens, it was well above my station to concern myself with the business structure of the gym. Who was I to have opinions?

I took my concerns to my manager, and it was explained to me that shower facilities cost money. There were issues in getting permits, finding the space, construction, maintenance—so many added costs that I hadn't even considered—and those costs just didn't make the cut when the budgets were laid out for these gyms.

Armed with an understanding as to why the showers hadn't been built, I could certainly see things from their end, but it still didn't make sense to me in the bigger picture. In my mind, the immediate costs were far outweighed by the long-term benefits of providing such a basic convenience to our clients.

Here you have a booming business that's tapped into a niche in the market with no signs of slowing down, and just as you're gaining momentum, you're willing to risk it all to the competitors at your heels by refusing to put in a shower stall? Talk about short-sighted vision! I pleaded my case, but at 17, it fell on deaf ears. So rather than dance in circles every time a client would ask about our showers, I did damage control instead.

While not every woman visiting our gym would inquire about shower facilities when they worked out – the issue definitely came up with new members – and I realized I had to be prepared.

I decided that my best approach was to hone in on each member's specific needs and try to better align their gym experience with the most convenient scheduling possible. I would suggest we develop a personalized workout schedule so that their morning workouts could be slated for weekends, or days when they would have the time to go home and shower afterward. For example, for weekday workouts, I would suggest coming in for an evening session after their workday was done, noting the gym would be less crowded and even jotting down of some exercise classes they might like during those hours. I would even offer them a free trial of certain evening classes, to entice them to give the after-work-workout idea a try!

I looked at things from an angle that would work to their benefit. These women were taking time from their no doubt busy schedules to come in and use our gym. Many of them were rushing in on their lunch hour, eager to fit a quick workout in mid-day, and I knew that if showering afterward became an issue, it might deter them from coming back.

Most of these women were already limited on time, so with my approach, I was able to present gym scheduling options that both offered them personalized service *and* bypassed the shower issue. It may not have been the ideal solution for every gym member, but it worked well enough to leave our clients thinking more about our positive approach to their needs and less about our lack of showers.

While my attempts to voice my opinion about the shower situation to my managers may not have been met with much enthusiasm, I managed to troubleshoot the issue on my own. Granted, it wasn't a permanent fix, but I learned the value in identifying a problem and working toward a solution. I might have given up after getting shut down on the issue by management, but instead I took it upon myself to be of value and get creative in my approach. I saw a problem—saw no fixed method for resolving it at my disposal and was forced to think outside the box for the answer. I couldn't install showers in our gym myself, I wasn't able to force the hand of management, and I also couldn't outright lie to our clients and tell them there were showers where there were none. So where did that leave me? It took some brainstorming, but eventually I arrived at the logic that while there may not have been reasoning behind the lack of showers that directly benefited our clients per se, that didn't mean I couldn't find some positive angle from which to approach it.

When you find yourself at a bump in the road and discover you're fresh out of ideas on how to get around it, take a step back and find another way. There is always another way. Have a vision, and then expand on it—and then expand on that. There are NO LIMITS—that's the motto of a true visionary—and one I recommend adopting.

Hard work and a creative spirit will take you further than you can ever imagine. You just need to begin by tapping into your own unique skillset and working from there. I found my niche in dealing with people and real estate. When you work, you make a living; but when you invest in real estate, that's where you can truly make a fortune. You won't need to dig too deep in our history books to find that countless fortunes have been amassed through real estate. With the rule of thumb being that property values tend to double every 7–10 years, the equity you put into property will no doubt in future be a safety net for yourself and your family.

When I found myself faced with hard times, a slow market and banks unwilling to lend me money, I began looking for alternative options. Leveraging myself by borrowing from private lenders allowed me to put my money into something that was solid and would continue to grow from the day I bought it. *Yes, you will pay a higher interest rate doing it this way, but the return is worth it!*

Ultimately, this growth would translate to more than I would have earned in one year's paycheque!

To me, the idea of investing in property has always been a no-brainer. Unfortunately, in our society today, the middle class seems to be disappearing, as the average price of a home continues to rise. This leaves our children with little hope of ever buying a home without help from parents or early investment planning. It's in times like these, where our middle class needs support to secure both their own and their children's futures, that we must be creative in our efforts to facilitate investment. It's no different than what we did in the '80s when interest rates skyrocketed. People still needed to buy and sell, and those in the business had to get creative in adjusting their sales tactics.

As the industry continues to expand its reach and access to new opportunities, it's important to continuously re-think and adapt our investment strategies to the times. I look at opportunities such as homes needing renovations, pre-construction homes, as well as condominiums—analyzing builder projects to see where I might be able to help in moving leftover inventory and completing sales. I am able to then develop new opportunities and incentives for buyers and investors. This in turn becomes a great way to build equity for buyers and get them into the market—a win-win for everyone involved!

When you talk about visionary spirit and wealth through investment, it's hard not to reflect on the story of one Canadian in particular who worked his way from impoverished beginnings to the very top of his industry. Fred De Gasperis immigrated to Canada from Italy as a teenager in the 1950s. Starting a small concrete business, he often worked 14-hour days, seven days a week to make ends meet. It was on such a day, at the tail end of a 14-hour shift, that he fell asleep at a construction site while operating a cement-finishing machine. Jerked awoke to the sight of his finishing machine spiraling off the edge of the 18th floor, Fred too, nearly followed from the open frame of the high-rise building's shell. You might think coming so close to death in an incident like that would leave a person reflecting on a new lease on life, but for Fred, his top priority was covering the cost of the machine he'd just watched plummet 18 stories to the ground!

All Fred had to his name in terms of assets at the time was an old truck, some tools and a small parcel of land. He would have to sell the land in a bid to cover his losses with the machine. When he discovered that the land sitting out in a remote community had in fact been amassing more value over the past year than he'd been making working 14-hour days on end, a light bulb went off. From thereon out, he bought as much land as he could, as often as he was able. Today, the De Gasperis name is synonymous with one of the largest landowners in Canada, and the once-small company is now one of the largest infrastructure companies in the world.

I once found myself desperate to establish some sense of security with no income and three children to support. Leveraging myself on the little bit of real estate I had, this became the first rung on a ladder that allowed me to climb out of a bad situation and begin securing a future for my children and myself. My little investment would double in value, allowing me to leverage myself to borrow against it and still retain my property.

The best path to laying the foundation for yourself and your family may not always be apparent at first. Often, the most lucrative opportunities can be found in the most unexpected of places. Expand on what you think you know, and always be willing to consider new ideas. Property investment may not be a new concept but finding innovative ways to benefit from this multi-faceted industry is one way in which modern-day visionaries are seeking to not just make a living but also make their fortunes.

CHAPTER FOUR

NEVER GIVE UP

Fall seven times and stand up eight.
—Japanese Proverb

Nothing you *do* is a failure. I repeat: *nothing you do is a failure.* It's the *not doing* that poses a problem—the sitting around waiting for life to happen, the wallowing in self-defeat, the "poor me" pity-party—*that's* the problem. I've said it before, and I'll say it again—if you're focused on your purpose, moving and doing things to get you closer to your aims, then you're not failing.

While we're on the subject, can we talk about that word for second? *FAILURE.* It's an ugly word, isn't it? I guess it goes with the ugly, discouraging feelings that tend to accompany it. I can't honestly say I know a single person who's ever accomplished anything without getting very familiar with the feeling of failure at least once on his or her journey.

Anyone who's ever tried to do anything with his or her life has stumbled—it's just a fact. No one gets the gift of smooth sailing, and thank God for that. Can you imagine if everything we ever tried went according to plan?

In 1968, scientist Dr. Spencer Silver was trying to develop a stronger-than-strong adhesive in his lab. His not-so-super glue was a dud, turning out instead as a low-tack reusable adhesive. Sensing potential in this accidental discovery, Silver spread the word to his employers at 3M Laboratories, but nothing came of it until 1974, when a colleague of his would come on board to help. The pair worked out the details of their prototype using yellow scrap paper from the lab next door (not their first choice in colour, but the only one available) to create the first stack of Post-It notes. They were first launched in 1977 with disappointing results, but 3M would try them out again in a different market the following year, finding great success and the start of what would become an internationally recognized product.

Try. Try again. That's the motto here. Had Dr. Spencer Silver seen his failure as a dead end, he might have chucked the glue in the trash and got back to work, never to realize the true potential behind his miscalculation. Can you imagine a world without Post-It notes?

Another innovator, Henry Ford, started chasing his dreams at a young age, spending all of his free time in a tiny shop he had equipped with machines to aid him in his creations. He would spend much of his early life between jobs before pursuing his true calling, and that journey wouldn't be without its dues. Ford would go broke several times under the failings of his early businesses before realizing the success he dreamed of with the Ford Motor Company. He is an icon in the industry, and a testament to the value in never giving up!

Famed designer and the first name in high-end bridal wear, Vera Wang might never have become who she is today if her original plans had panned out. Wang, a competitive figure skater in her youth, failed to make it onto the 1968 Olympic team, subsequently switching gears and taking a job as an assistant with fashion magazine Vogue in the early 1970s. She stayed on with the magazine for 15 years as a senior editor, all the while looking like a solid contender for the position of editor-in-chief. When she got passed over for the job, Wang again had to re-work her plans; she left the publication for what would ultimately prove to be her true calling. Today, Vera Wang is a fashion brand known and respected worldwide!

It seems to be an unwritten rule of business that before you can ever meet success, you've got to buddy-up with failure. Think of failure as the middleman to your dreams—the go-between that's got the inside track on what you'll need to get you where you aim to go. Failure may sound like a buzz kill, but really, he's the life of the party. He knows what will and won't work, and if you listen carefully, he'll be happy to tell you.

In 2008, I was asked to head a capital campaign for a charity near and dear to my heart—a foundation that aims to help women and children who've been victims of domestic abuse. This charity was built around the principles of helping others and making a positive impact in our community and abroad. Now, for all the help they'd given others, they were in immediate need of some themselves. They needed a new shelter and asked if I could I help. There was no doubt in my mind that I needed to be a part of this, as their cause touched me on a very personal level. Many of the women and children who benefited from shelters like this one came from varying backgrounds and formed part of our society's most vulnerable members. This has always been an important issue to me, particularly as domestic abuse is something I have myself witnessed firsthand.

At one point as a child, when my family first moved to Canada from Italy, we lived in a multi-family home. My siblings and I would often find ourselves in the company of the other families who lived with us as we waited for our parents to come home from work. The communal living situation might not have bothered me had it not been for some of the things I saw and heard at that time. I vividly recall being perched at the top of the stairs, holding onto the banister and peering down as the voices and cries from the people below would grow louder. Even at that young age, I understood what was going on. I would sit there, waiting for the sounds to fade, knowing that the silence would be a good indicator that the dust had settled.

These occasions of violence happened only when our parents were not home, and though I never discussed it with them, these memories have stayed with me, hauntingly, my whole life. To bear witness to abuse in any form is not something you forget. I began early on in my career lending support to families in similar situations. So, when the capital campaign came up, it was an easy decision—of course I would help.

Almost immediately after I got on board with the charity's capital campaign, the market crashed worldwide, marking a recession the likes of which hadn't been seen since the 1930s. Needless to say, I was thrown for a loop. I worried about my business, the severe impact that the market's downturn would inevitably have on the industry, the toll this would take on my ability to provide for my own family, the livelihood of the families of my agents, and now, my ability to do right in my new role with this charity.

I felt pulled from all angles. As far as my original plans for the charity, I knew that it would be even more difficult to knock on the doors of the usual crowd during such instability. This was a time when people were looking to sustain and stay afloat; it was survival mode across the board. I felt momentarily overwhelmed as the weight of everything on my shoulders began to settle in.

I realized nothing good could come by crumbling under the pressure. So, I got moving. Yes, the market had crashed, but, no, the world had not yet stopped spinning on its axis. Bills were still coming in, my agents and I still had families to feed, homes were still standing, waiting to be bought and sold, and the foundation I had signed on to help was still home to women and children whose need was greater than my own—women and children who were in desperate need of this new shelter. I would not let them down.

In terms of business, I reminded my team that our ability to persevere during challenging times was primarily a product of our own efforts; we were not solely reliant upon the market forecast. We determined how rainy a day, or year, it would be, and as far as I could figure, the sun was due out any day now.

My role in the campaign would be a harder one to tackle than originally anticipated, but I kept the merit of the cause at the forefront of my mind. I had signed on to help make a difference, and the nature of the market would not hinder my passion for the cause. I felt an immense sense of responsibility for coming through on my commitment. It would take me longer than initially projected, but I would make good on my promise, and my dedication to the cause would eventually be met with the kind of positive impact I had envisioned for this worthy foundation.

I was in a position where the thought of giving up just wasn't an option. Is it ever, really? Is it ever feasible to consider throwing up your arms and walking away from whatever it is you're after? If you can honestly answer "yes," then maybe you haven't been going after the right things. When you're working toward something that truly means something to you, the personal significance will be the thing that helps you withstand every trial that comes your way. This is why it's so vital to always be, in some way, working toward your purpose and contributing somehow to a greater good; goals of real substance will help sustain you through the hard times.

You can do anything you want to *besides* quit. If I had thrown in the towel on my commitments, I would have never forgiven myself. My dedication and passion for the tasks at hand were so strong that when the challenges began to mount, I only became more focused and more driven. Everything I was working toward played to my need to live out my purpose; all of it was in sync with who I am, and what I feel most passionate about. Think about it: I wasn't just looking to ensure the success of my business or keep a promise to the foundation—it went much deeper than that!

For my family, I was working to ensure our security and future. For my business, I had the wellbeing of my team in mind, the drive toward keeping us afloat for the sake of our livelihoods and the financial independence I'd been seeking for so long. As for the capital campaign, this was rooted in my need to support something that contributed to the greater good of our community, a cause that deeply impacted me at the core.

Set your sights on things that go beyond superficial values and refuse to let the obstacles in place deter you. When you elect to take yourself out of a losing equation and a negative mindset, you win. Maybe not every time, and almost never right away, but ultimately, you win. Never lose patience. When it comes to your happiness, you should always play the long game.

Bet on yourself, every time. Never see the race as having anyone but you in it, and never set a timer on your dreams. When you pit yourself against the clock, coupled with the pressure of keeping up with others, you put focus where it doesn't need to be. Fixing your attention on things that you can't possibly control will only ever distract you from what you should be focusing on—YOU.

Let's be very honest with ourselves for a moment. This idea of quitting, at its core, comes down to who you are and who you want to be. Are you someone who's tried, failed and given up in the past? That's ok, no judgment here, just own it.

What I've learned is that failure doesn't always have to be met with the grim reaper of goals; no one but you can take an axe to your dreams unless you say so. Nothing—I repeat, NOTHING—is dead in the water until you deem it to be.

This road you're headed down, this journey toward living out your true purpose, it's going to rise up on you and surprise you at every turn. It's a path few have taken, so there are sure to be all kinds of bumps in the road and potholes waiting to greet you.

Expect the unexpected. Anticipate the storms, because they're coming. You can either pack an umbrella and an open mind, or stay home and watch the show from the sidelines, but front and centre is the only place to be when the skies clear.

Giving up, or the *idea* of quitting, will never completely leave your psyche. We're all just human, and every one of us has the ability to bend until we break—to give in, to quit. No one is immune to the temptation, but we all have within us the ability to persevere. You need to look inward in those darker moments and come out fighting for what you want. Even with your back against the wall, when it feels like the world is caving in, you have everything you need to make it through.

Work with what you have, always investing in yourself. And if you find you aren't happy with who you are at present, give yourself permission to move forward and set your sights on the person you want to become.

No one is born destined to fail. Some are gifted with earlier opportunities than others, some are handed weights just as soon as we can hold out our hands and many of us will get our share of both blessings and burdens at varying points in our lives. These are the facts. We all come from different places. Some people, when asked what went wrong in their lives, will cite environmental factors as the cause. Maybe they were born in an area devoid of opportunity, where their chances for success were always, seemingly, out of reach. Other people will note financial factors as the cause of their failings—a lingering debt that just always seemed to stunt their chance for growth. Then there are those with emotional anchors: a broken family, a crippling domestic situation, others dependent on them—reasons to play it safe and avoid the uncertainty that comes with chasing your dreams.

None of these factors are negligible, and I'm not here to downplay anyone's life situation. God knows I've found myself at the centre of countless scenarios where it seemed life had just positioned me for hard times. But there's something you should know—I have *never* felt sorry for myself. Self-pity was never an indulgence I was interested in, and it shouldn't be for you, either. Yes, there were moments of doubt and countless sleepless nights, but I never for one second took the time and exerted the energy on making myself a victim. Giving up is easier if you convince yourself you are simply a victim of circumstance. This is a lie we tell ourselves to justify quitting. We give ourselves this role of victim, and that in turn gives us an "out."

When my acne flared up as a teen, I had a choice. I could either become an introvert and shy away from life, or GET MOVING and change my circumstances. When my house was foreclosed on and my dreams for my family crushed, I felt the fear and humiliation, sure, but I didn't crawl under a rock and give up on life. I packed our bags and moved on, treating it instead as a fresh start. When my office was sold, and I was left fighting for my livelihood, I found my inner strength and got to work, using whatever I had. As everything else life had to offer came hurtling my way, I learned to swallow my pride, dust myself off and do what had to be done to change my situation.

This is the thing—and this is important—so pay attention:

The world is *not* out to get you.

You are not at the centre of some universal plot to destroy your chances for happiness. Stop being paranoid, give up on the superstitious beliefs and get real!

The world and the people in it are *not* out to get you. Quite honestly, I think they all have better things to do. By engaging in these delusions, the only one plotting against you and standing in your way is you! All the procrastination, the fear, and the excuses—it all comes down to YOU. And if this is how you've been living, then you're doing a great job of stopping yourself short. In the story of your life, the only one with a conspiracy theory is you. I call it self-sabotage.

Your best chance of happiness lies out here in the real world where the person most accountable for your life's circumstance is you. Take control of how things are going, be responsible for your state of affairs, and if it's not to your liking, start making some changes. Stop procrastinating by playing the blame game or looking outward for the answers as to why things didn't work out. The past is the past, and while there's much to learn from looking at it, you can't expect to stay there and still move forward. Be present, be proactive and keep your head up and eyes forward. That's where your future is, always just ahead of that next step. There's always light at the end of the tunnel, you just have to put one foot in front of the other and get moving.

It may not seem like it now, but when you find yourself with the odds stacked against you, here is where you'll find your strength. Here is where it counts. In the moments that have you stretched so thin, reaching for that last ounce of clarity amidst the fog—here is where you discover what you're truly made of. This is where you'll shine.

Once upon a time, I blinked and found myself in the position of being a young wife and mother. These were heavy roles to play for someone with so little life experience and, at that time, no solid financial independence. Again, I felt an internal war brewing between the person I once was, and the one I had become in an effort to keep everyone else happy, and succeed at the things that were expected of me. I was torn, at a crossroads, desperate to take myself out of park and get moving towards a different direction, but at the same time plagued with guilt. Guilt is a killer. It will seep into your mind and rot your gut. It will fog your vision and leave you feeling helpless, stuck between what you *want* to do and what you feel you *should* do.

I hate to play the gender card here, because I truly believe both sides of the fence feel their share of inherent guilt, but there's no denying that the added pressure of juggling roles as a single mother and a woman in a male-dominated industry was one of the major constants that have followed me through all the ups and downs on my journey.

As a woman, I feel we are born with this inherent sense of female responsibility; we have an onus rooted in tradition that has us steered toward nurturing roles. Our present society, however, is at conflict with that, because so much of what we are exposed to today is geared at breaking down the idea of these traditional parts. So, how do we do it? How do we juggle being both the homemaker and the breadwinner? Somehow, as is evident by the countless women thriving and making new waves in business today, we manage. But it isn't without its due, as we find ourselves more burdened than ever with that sense of immeasurable guilt that has us feeling damned if we do, and damned if we don't.

I believe this is why so many women—and men— give up on their dreams; the weight of their guilt from wanting to live an authentic life is at odds with the consideration for who they may be letting down in doing that. But you simply can't let other people's issues and insecurities become your own, or you'll end up molding your life after the expectations of others.

Believe me when I tell you, this is the surest way to wake up one day filled with regret. The very idea of breaking tradition and stepping into new territories will naturally have you feeling as though something, somewhere in your life, must be suffering. It's understandable. Something's got to give, right?

As a stay-at-home mom during this time, I operated in an almost systematic way. I was so busy that there wasn't much time to feel like anything in my life was missing. How could I, when there was barely a moment to take a pause? And yet, there was this nagging sensation buried deep down, something telling me that, despite all the good things in my life, I needed to make some changes. My lack of financial freedom, the feelings of inadequacy that came with having to ask for things for my children and myself—all of it left me reflecting on the Vivian that I had put in park. This was not what I had envisioned for myself.

The only thing worse than the guilt I felt during that time was the guilt that followed my divorce. Here I was, a woman from a Catholic-European background, with three children, going through the dissolution of my marriage. I felt isolated as a failure in the eyes of my family. It wasn't so much what they said as what they didn't say. I knew what was going through their minds. I had gone against the values instilled in me from my youth. I was a black sheep.

All of a sudden, my role had changed; I was now a divorcee. I no longer fit the social circle I'd once had. What did we even have in common now? People I once looked to as friends would now go out of their way to avoid me. It was as though I'd been exiled from my own life. The guilt mounted as once-routine situations now had me feeling judged by the silent looks that spoke volumes above words. I felt the weight of it all pulling me downward, the sensation of now being an outsider in my own world.

In moments like these, when you find yourself feeling lost and in need of support, there tends to be a weakness and real vulnerability that follows. You become more susceptible to making poor choices as your judgment becomes blurred. It's in these times that you can find yourself caught up in the wrong "misery loves company" crowd—but it's so important that you see these bad influences for what they are: toxic and temporary. They may make you feel good for a short while, but that soon fades.

It felt like a dark time for me as I looked to regain my self-confidence, working through my guilt and the new roles I was set to play. I won't sugarcoat it, life isn't always going to be an easy climb, and some of the hard parts are going to impact you more greatly than others. There's no shame in finding yourself in a bad place, with everything seemingly out of whack all around you. It's okay, you're only human, and you're allowed to stumble and fall. But this shouldn't ever deter you from finding your way back up onto your path. There's no place in which you can't climb out from and be better for having experienced. There's always hope at the end of the tunnel, but it's up to you to get past those feelings of defeat and snap out of it!

My guilt at this time could have crippled me, but I chose instead to keep focused on my three children. It's that focus, strength and perseverance that I credit so much to my parents' example, which kept me on the course I needed to be on in challenging times.

Your happiness is always worth it. Mistakes will be made and setbacks are inevitable, but if you set your sights on better circumstances and start taking steps toward seeing it through, it will happen. You just have to keep moving. You're not going to wake up every morning feeling motivated to get back into the daily grind, especially at the start. But you've got to force yourself to get beyond that and approach each day with the determination to *do something* that will get you closer to your goals. *Anything.* Do things to get yourself in motion, always setting your sights on long-term goals substantial enough to keep you inspired.

Never give up on your dreams. Everyone is deserving of a life of purpose. You need to own that, and want it for yourself. Accept that nothing worthwhile has ever come easy, and rise to meet the challenges knowing you've done everything you could to prepare yourself at every turn. Not every day is going to be a good day, but you have everything you need to dust yourself off and get back on track. The struggle makes you stronger, and when you finally find yourself living out your authentic life, every hurdle it took to get you there will have been worth it.

CHAPTER FIVE

RELY ON YOURSELF

I didn't get here by wishing for it or hoping for it, but by working for it.

—Estée Lauder

In my world, the buck stops with me. I'm very fortunate to work with a phenomenal team—so many fine-tuned working parts involved in every aspect of our day-to-day operations—but ultimately, in my business, the buck stops with me.

I learned a long time ago that relying on myself first and foremost was the only way to get things done. If I wanted something, it was up to me to go out and get it. If I wanted changes made, I had to lead the movement and see it through. It was my responsibility to follow through on my plans and make it happen. Flash forward to present day and this rule still applies. My personal success is dependent on me and me alone. This is a mentality I have instilled in my children and do my best to reiterate to the people on my team every day. You have to take full responsibility for your life! Then, and only then, can you aim to take control of it.

Your best life is out there for the taking, but you've got to get out there and take it! A strong team is the foundation for success, yes, but before you can hope to lead a team, you've got to be able to do it for yourself. If personal success is by design, it only makes sense that you've got to know every inch of it for yourself before you can properly delegate to others. Knowledge is power, but only if you're aware of how to properly use it. Without an understanding of what it is you're after, it's like the blind leading the blind. Be conscious at every step and be very clear about what you want—specificity is key, and often, this clear vision of what you're after will be the only constant on your journey.

In business, as it is in life, your world and the people in it will be ever-changing as you grow and extend your reach. It's a bitter truth that the people you start out with will not always be the ones you finish with. That's just the way it is. People will come in and out of your life in varying capacities, but the only one true fixture is you. It's a tough lesson to learn, but you have to develop a real comfort with yourself, a real taste for solidarity, before you can ever aim to successfully lead a team.

Yes, a great leader knows when to delegate, but that same leader must also know how to navigate any obstacle and pick up the slack when needed. Beyond this, self-reliance is about being proactive in everything you do, approaching each situation with open eyes and ears, looking beyond what's in front of you and doing your due diligence to effectively read between the lines. The fine print in every situation is up to you to decipher—and believe me, there's always fine print!

I learned this lesson some years ago when a business acquaintance of mine, a fellow broker, came to me with a proposal—or rather, a life or death proposition. The situation was this: his spouse was terminally ill, essentially on her last breath, and they desperately wanted to sell their company to me to free up both the time and peace of mind they needed to take care of what mattered most. At our first meeting, my initial reaction was to ask for some time to think it over. At our second, he pleaded further, adamant that I was the only one they trusted in this situation, distraught, as anyone would be, at the thought of losing his spouse. Could I help, he implored, could I come through for them in this way, the only person they felt they could trust with this?

Talk about knowing me—he hit all the right notes!

How could anyone turn down someone who is grappling with a spouse on their deathbed and the weight of everything that would follow? To know that I was the only one they trusted with this, well, it goes without saying that I couldn't possibly take that sentiment lightly. So, I agreed to do it. The very moment I said yes, it seemed the deafening sounds of an orchestra kicked up all around me and everything began to fast-forward from there, launching my world into chaos by the events that would follow.

Much to their advantage, this fellow broker had a background in banking. Initially, this gave me some assurances as to the financials involved and the validity of the numbers to come. I shouldn't have felt quite so assured.

Coincidentally, around the same time the sale closed, so did the steady stream of the grieving broker's tears. From there, everything moved at warp speed as I learned firsthand just how quickly things could go wrong. My gut was telling me something wasn't right, but the wheels were already in motion. Once the press release went out, there was no way to turn back the clock, and by the time I got the financials . . . Well, I guess sometimes one plus one equals three? I felt that sinking feeling in my gut as I finally understood just how I had been played from day one.

My lawyer advised me to cut the cord, but how would it look, on my end, to sever ties with this well-respected broker? I had made a commitment; I couldn't just go back on my word.

The dizzying sounds of the symphony that seemed to be playing in the background grew steadily louder as I struggled to hear my own thoughts. The broker had hit all the right notes with me from the start. He'd known just what to say, his true intentions having been cleverly veiled by what had looked to me to be sincere grief and desperation. By the time I found myself in court, I was far less prepared than the other side. Coupled with the frenzied sounds of an orchestra still echoing overhead, I was reminded of that scene in court from the movie-musical *Chicago*. You know the one, where the music starts as lawyer Billy Flynn strikes up his defense, a dazzling display of cunning misdirection, all to the sounds of tap and jazz.

In the film, the other side never saw it coming—and neither did I.

I got a crash course in the court process, and while it was less than thrilling to watch my lawyer struggle to keep the beat, I took away much more than I lost. The experience was a game-changer for me, a million-dollar lesson that I'd never forget.

On the bright side of things, you'll be happy to know—*miracles do happen!* The broker's spouse, who, as her story went, had been standing at the brink of death, made a full recovery just as soon as the trial ended . . . Hallelujah!

Ultimately, there's no denying I got the wool pulled over my eyes because someone knew me well enough to appeal to my better nature. But like anything else, you have to seek out the positive in every situation, and believe it or not, there was a lot of that to be taken from this one. Armed with the lessons this afforded me, I've been able to share my experiences with other people who come to me for guidance.

My hindsight can now be the foresight for someone else, something that has proven beneficial to that effect many times over. I've been able to help others in seeking alternative measures when necessary, warning them against knee-jerk reactions, advising them to filter through the issues with a clear head and never neglecting to mention that, regardless of the money at play, it's the emotional energy you just can't get back when you make the wrong moves.

I had been left with a costly lesson that would be paid by leveraging it against myself, but it was the emotional exhaustion from standing at the centre of a storm that had me eager to get back on my feet and continue moving forward. More than the money, it was the time and energy invested that took me the longest to recover. Instead of feeling sorry for myself, I focused on the positive and was able to see the value in the lessons I now had in hand. These would help get me back to my feet, and prove to be of immeasurable value in the future. You're going to take your lumps in business and in life, but these will be the lessons that will serve a purpose. You can always recuperate—you can always bounce back!

Relying on yourself is about being your own safety net. At present, I have over 1,000 agents working for my companies and I oversee 60 employees out of 12 offices. At every level, everyone's role is important and specific to their skillset. Many of these roles are ones that I would in no way myself qualify as an expert. However, if push came to shove, I'm confident that my team and I are fully capable of stepping up with a plan or, at the very least, some temporary solution. Knowing the ins and outs of your business is crucial to becoming a successful leader. It grants you the knowledge of knowing what questions to ask, the ability to see the warning signs, and the capacity to step in when needed. I would not function at this level without my team, but if it called for it, I am certain in my ability to do the appropriate damage control in every sector.

That's the role of a leader—to perform wherever needed, but at the same time to recognize the indisputable value of a team that can operate in its own right. Never be so short-sighted as to think you know it all. Surround yourself with professionals who know more than you when it comes to decisions in the legal and financial realm. These are some of the areas where you will need the most support as a leader; so, make sure you have the right people in place.

It's about more than being able to oversee the things happening around you. It's about being confident enough in your own skin to make decisions and voice opinions that may not be popular with anyone but you. It's about making moves that might leave you standing out and apart from the crowd, but being solid enough in your convictions to know that your resolve is enough. Relying on yourself isn't just a skill, it's SURVIVAL. How can you expect to make your mark, much less succeed in your goals, if you can't count on yourself? How can you ever hope to assemble and lead a team, if you lack the confidence in your own abilities?

My learning curve in this arena started early in life, as it was clear that what was expected of me just didn't gel with the expectations I had in mind for myself. I may not have understood the driving force behind it at the time, but I did sense the urgency in establishing my independence. It's this do-it-for-yourself attitude of mine that saw me through the harshest of critics, a broken marriage (and even more broke bank account), career advances that always seemed just a hair out of reach and every ensuing shot to the gut after that which required me to stand on my own two feet and do what needed to be done.

I'm no superhero, and I make no qualms about admitting my weaknesses—but I also know my strengths, and I've learned to give myself more credit than I once did and trust in my own capabilities. If something needs to be done, I know I can do the work to make it happen. I have spent a lifetime looking inward for solutions, and despite the hills and valleys, I feel it's only ever worked in my favour. I attribute much of my success to working from within, something that has always been rooted in my sense of not only independence but also responsibility.

The concept of responsibility, for most anyhow, starts young. You're given tasks and are responsible for completing them. You're assigned homework and are responsible for finishing it on time, or you've begun your first job and are responsible for performing the duties required, and so on and so forth. As you get older, these responsibilities become not only more challenging but also more closely connected to your goals. Being responsible for yourself in adulthood goes beyond simply doing what's expected of you, because there will be times when, *even when you do your part*, unforeseen factors will come into play and throw a wrench in your plans. So, then what? What happens when you discover that something outside of your control is weighing you down?

Not all of us were born into financial stability. Not all of us found great success in school, despite our best efforts. Not everyone has been fortunate enough to find their way in life with a supportive network of people behind them. Some of us found ourselves faced with environmental, emotional or financial roadblocks early on. Everyone has their own story and individual starting point.

There's really no end to the varying challenges and circumstances that people have faced and will no doubt continue to encounter in the future.

So, how do you cope? How do you move forward in spite of what you might perceive as your shortcomings holding you back? Well, I'll tell you:

YOU DO EVERYTHING IN YOUR POWER TO USE WHAT YOU'VE GOT TO MAKE IT WORK!

You may be at a stage of your life where you're not exactly where you'd hoped to be—so what? Maybe your career hasn't quite taken off like you'd envisioned. Perhaps your relationships haven't been as satisfying as you'd anticipated. Maybe your bank account seems a few zeros short of what you'd imagined. Again, so what?

THIS is your starting point: now, today, THIS MOMENT! Consider everything you aren't happy with as your base, the jumping off point—a slate to wipe clean and build from.

Where you're starting from may not be by choice, but where you find yourself tomorrow is. For most people, it's taken hard work and concentrated effort to find a sense of peace and satisfaction with who they are and what their true purpose is. No one comes off the assembly line as a finished product in this life, and it's only to your benefit to understand that you, me—every one of us—are forever a *work in progress*. Where you might feel you don't measure up, there's undoubtedly some other aspect of yourself that more than makes up for it—so focus on that!

Focus on what you have, not what you feel you lack. Nurture your strengths and use those inherent tools to help build up the areas you feel need improvement, but never lose sight of the immense value in your own unique composition. It's the signature design of who you are that is going to be your greatest strength, flaws and all. Never put off to tomorrow what you can do today because you feel you aren't "at that level" or that you don't measure up to others. You *are* enough. You certainly have enough to, at the very least, get started. Do something. Do *anything*. Start NOW!

You've got to take FULL CONTROL of your life. After all, it is *yours*—it may not be what you ordered, but it's what you've got, so do the best with it—every single inch of it. The good, the bad, the ugly, the whole enchilada. Got it? Good!

This is YOUR LIFE. Get over any feelings of resentment and ill will, they're just bricks that will slow your stride—and make peace with them. Don't carry resentment around like a packed suitcase; it will only weigh you and everyone around you down. Your life is up to you, and only you. The responsibility is yours to do with your life what you will. That's the truth of it, so the sooner you stop dwelling on it, the sooner you can get back on track and move forward. There's no excuse to avoid getting started on living your authentic life. There's no trait you might lack that would justify putting yourself and your happiness in park.

Being responsible for yourself is a big part of growing into the person you want to be, because those are some big shoes to fill, and you're going to have to pay your dues like anyone else. Self-fulfillment is hard enough to come by, let alone aspiring to lead others, and you're going to have to get comfortable with the idea that it all comes back to you. This isn't all bad—the accolades and praise are a part of that; but, often, this means that when someone else drops the ball, it's on you to step up and kick into resolution mode.

People who refuse to hold themselves accountable are the same people who will never fully be able to rely on themselves. They come up with every excuse in the book and never seem to run out of reasons why it just wasn't their fault. As a rule, I don't have anyone like this on my team—and you shouldn't either. You should expect from others what you have come to expect from yourself—which, hopefully, includes the very important trait of accountability.

The ability to be responsible for yourself and to recognize how your role influences the performance of others and so many other aspects of your business—particularly in terms of *trust* and *growth*.

Being a leader means having a team that trusts you enough to follow by your example. How can you expect them to be confident in your leadership if they can't anticipate just what falls under your jurisdiction? For example, if you-know-what hits the fan, can they trust that you will stand at the front lines for them, every time?

And what about growth? No enterprise can hope to grow or expand without someone at the helm who's willing to own not only their successes, but their shortcomings as well. You need to be able to take the lion's share and work from there, otherwise you may as well just move to the back of the line and let someone else take the lead.

Believing in yourself enough to become your own go-to takes some work, but it's there within you: allow it to come out. Knowing you can count on yourself, and emitting the confidence to rally others, means you need to bring everything you can to the table to assure both yourself and those around you that you're prepared for whatever may come. Did you catch that word? *PREPARED*.

No one is born with everything they need to thrive in business—or in life, for that matter. You've got to do the work and seek ways to fill the voids where you find them. Educate yourself where you feel ignorant about a subject, and come prepared every time. The onus is on you as to where you direct your focus. I can't emphasize enough how important it is to constantly seek ways to grow, learn, and improve upon existing skills—not to mention strategizing ways to develop new ones. This might mean furthering your education in some way, seeking out the advice of a mentor or someone in your field—whatever it takes to learn your craft. Remember: growth is a constant, and opportunities to learn and improve are the ones that will help mold you into someone who is capable of not only relying on yourself, but also of inspiring others to follow your lead.

Speaking of inspiration, I draw a lot of that from people whose stories resonate with me. One in particular that really zeroes in on this idea of relying on oneself and harnessing knowledge is the story of Henry Ford's libel suit against the *Chicago Tribune*. In an article written about him, Ford had come under heavy scrutiny, being labelled an "anarchist" and "ignorant man," amongst other things. This was too much for the famed manufacturer, so Ford took the paper to court in 1919 in a libel suit for $1,000,000. With no shortage of legal representation on either side, both parties came to court prepared for what would turn out to be a lengthy and legendary battle of wits.

This trial was also famously re-examined for its influence on our perception of what it meant to be an educated man at the time. In Napoleon Hill's 1937 classic, *Think and Grow Rich*, Hill shed light on an issue that went well beyond name-calling and allegations of slander in journalism to get to the core message surrounding traditional views of intelligence.

In an effort to defend their claims, the *Chicago Tribune* put Ford on the stand and subjected him to lines of questioning so ridiculous, that jurors likely felt as though they were witnessing a pop quiz in historical fact rather than a trial.

Hoping to prove Ford's ignorance and establish that their claims had merit, Ford was asked countless general knowledge questions relating to the times. Everything from politics to major historical figures and anything else the defense deemed to be something an "educated" man should know.

Henry Ford took no one by surprise when he was unable to answer most of what was being asked of him, but the shock for those in attendance came once he finally grew tired of the questions and turned the tables on the papers' attorneys. Ford explained to the court that while he may not have the answers to their questions, he was able, by the push of a button in his offices, to find them via someone under his employment that he had hired for exactly that purpose! His education, while not obtained in the traditional sense, was extensive via his mastery in his field. His intelligence was harnessed in specificity to his business. It was from there that he credited having the foresight to be intelligent enough to employ people who could pick up the slack for things that were outside of his immediate focus.

The logic behind this is brilliant: Ford understood the value in focusing his efforts on where they could be of best use, and assigning the right resources to be available for everything else. It wasn't as though he felt these other areas were unimportant; rather, he knew he needed to reserve his concentration for his business, and so he covered his bases by keeping those who knew what he didn't at arm's length. Talk about foresight!

The trial lasted three months. When it was all said and done, it took jurors just over ten hours to come back with their verdict. The *Chicago Tribune* was found guilty of libel against Henry Ford. The judge who had presided over the trial emphasized that it was clearly not monetary compensation that Ford had sought in his lawsuit—both sides having lost quite a bit over the course of the proceedings—but that Ford had obviously sought to be vindicated over a more important issue.

No one can expect to be an expert at everything. This is why, when discussing the concept of achieving one's goals and working toward a purpose, there is such an emphasis on being *specific*. Henry Ford was not a genius in the scholastic sense, but he was a brilliant pioneer in the way of a man who knew better than to try to do it all himself.

While not everyone is able to enlist a team to stand behind them to help cover all their bases, what I took away from Henry Ford's story is that we are all able to harness our own form of education by finding our best focus and having conviction in our methods. By trusting in your vision and narrowing things down so that they are manageable, anyone can work to become an expert in his or her field. Regardless of whether or not you have had extensive formal schooling or look "good on paper"—YOU are in control of your own intelligence. You control to what and where your energy goes, so be selective—and know when to ask for help.

Here I am with my mother and sister in
Italy. We are on our way to get our
passport photos taken to come to Canada.

On the *Queen Frederica* en route from Italy to Halifax.

MARINA ITALIAN CLUB
Presents
THE ELECTION OF
MISS ITALIA ETOBICOKE 1970
Dancing with
The Orchestra of "THE MORENAS SIX"
and PINO PAPA *(singer)*

MISS ITALIA ETOBICOKE WILL
PARTICIPATE AUTOMATICALLY
IN THE MISS ITALIA CANADA
CONTEST WHICH INCLUDES A
FREE TRIP TO ITALY BY:

CPAir
Canadian Pacific
FLIES NON-STOP TORONTO ROME

Vivian Fusco Miss Etobicoke 1969

Admission
men *$2.50*
girls free

MEMBERS OF THE
"MARINA ITALIAN CLUB"
WELCOME FREE

TICKETS ALSO AVAILABLE
AT THE DOOR

YORK CENTRE BALLROOM
611 VAUGHAN RD. (near Oakwood)

SUNDAY APRIL 12   8:00p.m.

For more information call :
Toto at 781—1034   or   Joe Garisto at 531 — 1117

As Miss Italia Etobicoke, getting ready to participate in Miss Italia Canada. I was 14 years old, passing myself off as a 16-year old. What was I thinking?

Meeting with the one-and-only Oprah Winfrey,
when she was in Toronto for a speaking event.
She is truly inspirational.

MC James Cunningham coming to my rescue when
I was introducing Tony Robbins at a speaking event
and had just been told he was running late.

On stage to introduce Tony Robbins at a
speaking event in Toronto, Ontario.

The inspiring Tony Robbins at a
speaking event in Toronto, Ontario.

With my children (left to right): Julie,
Justin, myself and Michelle.

Away with the family for 60th birthday.
(Left to Right): Matthew, Justin, Lisa &
Sofia, Jim, Elias, Michelle & Alexandra,
myself, Victoria, Julie, Jonathan, & John

With the visionary entrepreneur Richard Branson.

CHAPTER SIX

FOLLOW YOUR INSTINCTS

Follow your instincts. That's where
true wisdom manifests itself.
—**Oprah Winfrey**

Follow your gut. Trust me on this.

In a world where everything can seem so loud and distracting, it's going to be your inner voice, and those finely tuned *instincts,* that will help you on your way.

It was 1994, and we were smack dab in the middle of a recession. The timing couldn't have been worse to start my company. But I felt strongly then, as I do now, that with a strong work ethic and by building a solid team, we would be able to come out on the other side with something to show for it. Giving up was never an option. This wasn't just a paycheque that hung in the balance; this was my *life.* It was survival—simple as that.

We were a small group, just me at the helm and 18 other realtors. There's no doubt I felt the pressure, but I refused to let my team see it. They needed a leader, and I was determined to give it everything I had. I used methods that fell well outside the norm at the time; where others were pulling back, cutting costs and playing it safe, I went the other way. I invested more, shelling out $5,000 (that I didn't have) for a six-week training course for my agents, at no cost to them. We converted our three offices, separated by folding doors, into one large conference room and set up long tables that would accommodate everyone. I brought in a trainer and made every effort to educate, train and empower my agents as a part of the team and in their own right.

I invested in my people and, in turn, my office tripled in size. We began to see the kind of early success that not only peaked the curiosity of competing brokerages, but also drew attention from an industry giant. When they came to me with an offer to buy my business, I was both flattered and petrified at the thought! I didn't need more than a moment to come back with my answer: NO.

This was *my* business, my hard-earned independence. More than that, I wanted this not just for myself, but for my family. I had three kids to consider. The responsibilities and needs of a growing family rested heavily on my shoulders. I wouldn't just be selling an office, I'd be handing over my livelihood, and there was no price they could put on that.

Undiscouraged, they came back with another proposal: they wanted *me* to buy *their* surrounding offices. They figured if our small office was not only sustaining but *thriving* despite being tucked between two of their offices, our direct competitors, *we* had to be doing something right, and they wanted in on it. This would mean that I would be doubling in size overnight—*Are you kidding me?* This was huge! I spent eight sleepless months grappling with an inner battle that had me struggling to shift from a mindset of "No way! I CAN'T!" to "I CAN!"

I had never visualized myself in this position. Like everything else that had surprised me on my journey thus far, the idea of taking on competing offices, rebranding on both ends and merging with what had so recently been our top competitors, fell well outside the plan I'd had in mind. This would be a game-changer, and while I hadn't expected it, I knew deep down that I had to do it. I had to give myself permission, knowing full well of course, that it wouldn't be easy. These were the competitors we'd been going head to head with for years. This kind of a merge would be like bringing together two families settled into their ways and undergoing big changes necessary to make it all work. I would be replacing an 80-year corporate ownership. Talk about a shift in gears for everyone involved! This was not going to go over very well with the people on both sides who hadn't signed up for such drastic changes. I thought to myself, *I guess we'd better brace for impact, and expect a few casualties!*

As I ran through the pros and cons in my mind, I began to see things more clearly, and my inner guide came into play. It was then that I realized that what I was struggling with was *fear of the unknown*, and not my inability or lack of skills in taking on this new challenge. If fear was the only thing keeping me from taking the plunge, it just wasn't a good enough reason. So, all my "no's" turned to a resounding "YES!" and I jumped headfirst into my next adventure knowing full well what tricky waters might lie ahead and understanding that I would need to be sure of myself and ready for anything in order to navigate them.

I struggled with thoughts of how it would be from the perspective of our competitors, as I went from rival to owner. There was no doubt in my mind that the acquired corporate offices would hate me, at least initially. And there were a lot of them! Here was their *direct competitor* suddenly switching roles from their adversary in business to their broker. That wouldn't be an easy pill to swallow for anyone. This had come as unexpectedly to me as it would for them. Was I ready to take on this responsibility and a complete shift in my original plan?

And just like that, the other side of my brain kicked in with, *So what if it's unexpected? Has anything else in your life happened on schedule or according to plan?*

No, it certainly hadn't.

I recognized what a challenge this would be. I was bringing my competitors on board, uniting rivals and was further tasked with the role of doing it all as "the boss." I would have to win them over, it was the only way. I knew that at the end of the day, the only person I had control over was myself, so I would have to be the one to step up as their leader and set the tone. Doing my best to lift the veil on the situation, I left my door open to the new members of our team, as I had always done with my own people. I let them know that I was there waiting to get to know them, that I was available to them. It was all about transparency and communication. They had to feel welcome. It was vital to me that everyone on board of our team felt confident, and it was up to me to instill that confidence.

Encouraging my new agents to get to know me, I took every opportunity to get to know them as well. It was crucial that they begin to see me as an ally. From my efforts, we soon began to build bridges in place of the walls we had broken down.

I had trusted my instincts, and everything grew from there. Sure, it could have been a disaster. I could have drowned under the weight of all that added responsibility and pressure—but I didn't. Honestly, I don't believe any of it had to do with luck. I was growing, learning to be confident in my abilities, sticking to my strengths and taking things step by step. I was a people person, and that's where I would start.

I understood that our industry, at its core, has always been a people business; beyond any fears I might have had, I was more than confident in my ability to rally this team towards a common goal. My instincts steered me past my doubt and landed me in a place where I could work from a positive mindset, with a fresh perspective rooted in working from my strengths.

I believe that we are all born with an inherited set of instincts. This spiritual inheritance, if you will, is one that's passed down to us from those who came before; a gifted sixth sense, even. From there, we take everything we learn as we go: all of our experiences, the things we are exposed to; the good advice of others (and the bad), it all contributes to that guttural voice that helps to steer us.

Getting in tune with this inner guide isn't always easy—it requires *listening*. We do so much talking and voicing over of our own thoughts each day, it's really incredible to consider just how little listening some of us actually do. You'd be amazed at what a little quiet reflection can help to accomplish if you only try!

I'm not about to push meditation on you (I promise!); I know that isn't for everyone, and to be honest, I'm not sure that what I do even qualifies as that. What I am going to suggest is the following: every day, at the very *end* of your day, carve out a little time for some light self-reflection. Simple, focused, reflection—no meditative chanting or incense necessary. Consider your day. Reflect on both your successes and the things you felt could have gone better.

Consider the day to come: What are your goals? What is your purpose, your driving force, for the next 24 hours of your life? How will you maximize those hours? Talk it out on your own if you have to, whatever it takes to make the most of this one-on-one time with yourself.

Most importantly, start—and finish—from a place of gratitude. When I reflect on the people I've met, the things I was able to do or the positive impact I may have had on someone else, I'm grateful for it all. Beginning and ending your personal reflection this way is a good technique to ensure you keep that positive energy and perspective at the forefront of your mind.

Getting on top of your thoughts will help clear out some mental inventory and facilitate the space to do a little listening. After all, once you've done all that thinking and self-communicating, what's left to do but listen? We often find it so difficult to tune into that little voice because we've got so much going on that our own anxieties drown it out. That little voice is an ally, but it's a soft-spoken one, so you're going to have to listen carefully if you want to hear it. Believe me, you'll want to hear what it has to say as you navigate your way, particularly in the choppy waters of business.

The real estate industry is constantly changing and evolving, and you have to keep yourself in sync with both the times and your own inner voice in order to stay afloat. When it comes to business, any business, you have to work to keep yourself informed. Do the research, be on your game, and never lose sight of who you are and what role you play in the bigger picture. This isn't easy to do; it's a delicate balance, keeping in tune with the world around you and also with yourself. With this in mind, it's easier to understand that whole 80/20 rule, isn't it? It is those select few who manage to zero in on that certain relationship between purpose and progress who will go on to become masters of their craft.

It's up to you to do your research and filter out fact from fiction and truth from true-*ish*. It's an unfortunate reality that not everyone in business, and life for that matter, has your best interests—or their clients'—at heart. Some people are only out for themselves, and in an industry that I believe is centrally rooted in people, you're doing yourself no favours by following their lead.

Good instincts, like a good nature, can't be taught. It really is both an inherent and time-developed skill. While I do believe that facts and precedent should lead decision-making, I know when to let my instincts have the final say. Believe me, as the stakes get higher, people out to pull the wool over your eyes will only get more creative—and you have to learn not to take everything at face value. A strong leader knows not just when to push forward, but also when to pull back.

For example, as a leader, I make a point of staying on top of current trends. If there's growth to be had by adapting to new methods or procedures in the industry, I ensure both my team and I are up to speed. As a rule, I do my research first and then make decisions to act. My instincts have always told me to take a back seat when it comes to jumping on board with of-the-moment business trends. The real estate industry is constantly in motion, and it's critical that I not only stay in the loop but also remain firm in my own principles.

The future of real estate may be limitless in its potential, but the history of this industry still has much to be learned from. Rooted in our past, this business has always been, even in its most rudimentary beginnings, at the forefront of our society. War, religion and the never-ending battle for power has always had land—the eternal driving force since the earliest of days—at its epicentre. An emotionally driven asset then as it is now; this business is both very real and very personal. While we may not be storming the castle gates over parcels of land in present day, that doesn't mean we are any less affected by the nature of this business.

At present, the purchase and sale of property remains one of the largest investments anyone will make in their life-time—How could that not be personal? In an industry so rich in history, and with so much on the horizon of its future, it really is the business that never quits. Somehow, in spite of all this, I manage (most nights) at least a few hours of sleep!

Trusting in myself and listening to my instincts have allowed me to work in and grow a business that feels more like an extended family than anything else. There's no way any of this would have been possible if I hadn't listened to my head, followed my heart, and let that inner wisdom within lead.

Go with what you know, and success will follow. Me, I understand people. This is one of my greatest strengths. I have a real sense about them, and I credit that to my experiences with past relationships, and also a good share of challenges along the way. This business fuels me, but make no mistake, it is a jungle out there, where the term "survival of the fittest" has never rung so true.

If there's anyone we can learn from in respect to instinct, survival and resiliency, it's our animal counterparts. Take the African savanna, for example, where every day is a do-or-die situation for the countless animals that live amongst those harsh and merciless plains. It's in this atmosphere that you'll find an advanced course in survival, as you look to the interchanging roles of predator and prey.

If I asked you to place your bet of survival on either the ferocious lion or the delicate gazelle, both savanna natives, which would you choose? With every skill of attack and strength in their favour, there's a good chance you'd put your money down on the lion. I don't blame you. Few animals are more deadly or dominant than the king of the jungle. With him on the hunt, the odds seem to be stacked against the gazelle.

But don't go writing off the underdog that quickly.

What you might not know, is that the gazelle harbours some of the best survival instincts in the animal kingdom. Beyond its grace and delicate features, the gazelle was built for speed, and more often than you might imagine, manages to avoid becoming a meal. What advantage the lion has in its ability to hunt and attack, the gazelle makes up for in endurance, a supercharge of adrenaline kicking up as the gazelle's nervous system readies it for the threat at hand. You probably never thought the gazelle stood a chance!

While real life for the rest of us doesn't play out on the plains of the savanna, there are many similarities between the interactions amongst animals and within the human world.

Many of us feel defeated before we even begin, discouraged at the thought of pitting ourselves against those we feel encompass the things we lack and the people we see as alphas. Feeding into self-doubt and believing we can never measure up, we shoot ourselves in the foot before we ever take that first step. Think again of gazelles, though, the underdogs in the fight against the hungry lions. Gazelles know what they're up against. They know the odds aren't in their favour—but do they roll over and give up? No way! Instead, gazelles work their own intrinsic skills to their benefit and give themselves an edge that can out-measure even the most lethal of opponents.

Use what you have and do everything in your power to live out your purpose and become the best version of yourself possible! Never let a lack of skills or resources keep you from being resourceful in your goals. Find your own way, use what you have as your jumping off point and build from there as you gather the experience and lessons along the way to help you grow as a person and a leader.

There is NO EXCUSE for giving up. With every bit of you invested in seeing yourself succeed, it's going to take more conscious effort for you to fail than it is to simply get in the game and GO FOR IT.

You need to build your philosophy on life around the idea that you are destined for greatness—that living out your authentic purpose is going to make a real difference in not just your life, but the lives of others. It's that sense of duty toward the greater good that will keep you engaged in positive thinking and in following your intuition. While your instincts are there to help guide you, they can't do it alone! You have to BELIEVE you are capable of achieving what you want, and what you want has to be substantial enough and relate heavily enough to your purpose to sustain your drive on even the worst of days. No one element can take you all the way to living your authentic and best life; you need to engage every natural resource you have at your disposal and WORK WHAT YOU HAVE TO THE FULLEST!

Don't let anything get in your way, and if what you need to do doesn't factor in with your original plans, then change your plans! Don't skip out on life because you forgot to mark it down on your calendar!

It isn't always fear or self-doubt that stunts our growth, either. Sometimes the limitations we put on ourselves come from a place of guilt, a concern for neglecting our responsibilities and obligations to others. We may worry how others who rely on us might suffer if we begin to focus instead on our own wants and needs. And so, we dutifully live out our lives, meeting the expectations of others as our driving force. We fail to realize that what we are doing is so far and apart from satisfying our true purpose that we might as well be trying to fill a glass with the bottom cut out. You'll always come up empty when you forget to factor yourself into the mix.

I spent four years as a stay-at-home mom, and I did everything I could think of to master the role as I understood it to be at that time. I baked until I could bake no more, crocheted to within an inch of my life and joined all the women's circle knitting groups I could find. I volunteered at my children's school and was first on the list to help with bake sales. I even subjected my family to what I affectionately refer to as my "Amish phase"—learning the craft of double-sided patchwork quilts and macramé as if my life depended on it. I trimmed bath mats, toilet mats, anything you can think of, to the point where my children began to fear I would trim them if they stood still long enough!

The point is—I was busy. In the moments where I felt I wasn't, I quickly found hobbies or tasks to fill those pockets of time as well. Yet, there was always a sense that something was missing. I hadn't taken the time to discover what, exactly, was out of place, but I *felt* it.

My days began at 6am and were packed until the moment I tucked in at night. I loved that time spent with my kids. Somewhere along the way, however, I had put myself in park and forgotten where I'd stored the key.

I mean, what did *Vivian* want? *Me*? Oh, that's right, I forgot about me!

It was as though there just weren't enough hours in the day to truly check in with myself. Every day like this seemed to weigh more and more heavily on my subconscious. Something had to change. I was torn between how I felt and how I knew I should feel. I asked myself, *Why do I feel this way? Why can't I just be happy like the other mothers? Why don't I fit in?* It was this internal conflict where my gut was telling me I needed change, but my head had all signs pointed to me being a failure as a mother. I just couldn't figure where I had gone so wrong to be feeling this way. *What was wrong with me that I couldn't feel the way everyone else seemed to?*

I thought back to my beginnings: I had started out in life with ambition, always looking to resolve my issues independently, looking to myself first for solutions. I was a self-starter who always felt a little out of place amongst my peers. I'd always been wise beyond my years and never pictured myself relying on anyone else to steer my life for me. When I became a wife and mother, the magnitude of these new roles set in. While trying to give my best to everyone around me, I put myself in park to better live up to the expectations before me.

When I started taking steps to reconnect with my authentic self, getting back in sync with what I consider my spiritually inherited instincts was a big part of that. It has always been a philosophy of mine that no matter what happens in your life, where the road takes you, how far you stray from your path, your inner guide is always there. Even if it falls dormant, like it did for me during that time, you can always come back to it when you're ready. This is what steadied me in the hardest of times—the knowledge that, deep down; I had the strength to persevere.

These inner instincts I'm talking about are a collective of your life's lessons—something within that evolves to further encompass your experiences as you grow. It doesn't matter where you come from, or what start to life you've had, everyone is born with his or her own set of instincts. Even if you were born in a box, you've still managed to experience parameters, a basis on which to gauge good and bad, right and wrong. Even if you forget along the way, this true sense of self never leaves you. It's more than just a "gut feeling," it's a survival guide that's uniquely your own, shaped by your life and everything within it. To access it, you only need to trust yourself.

It's interesting, isn't it, that when we have a question that we can't seem to find the answer to, we look to a book, type it into Google, or ask someone else; we trust that somewhere *out there* lies the answer. We find it so much more plausible that someone else might know better or more than we do. So, we look out when often we should be looking in. As a result, the answers we get are often not as tailored to our needs as we might have liked. We wonder what's wrong with us, doubting ourselves yet again.

If you want the right answers, you need to ask the right questions. For that to work, you need to be looking within when you start asking. Trust yourself enough to look inward for direction when it comes to living your life fully and getting the results you seek. If you doubt yourself at every turn, you'll end up following the herd instead of leading it. Even if you're comfortable with the idea of letting someone else lead, be wary that they aren't leading you right off the cliff.

This reminds me of a particular scene in the film, *Far from the Madding Crowd*, in which a shepherd's new sheepdog herds his entire flock of sheep right off a cliff, leaving him penniless and his flock dead. There was something about that scene and the parallels it represents to our own willingness to follow without question that was so impactful to me. You need to be aware of where you're headed and who's setting the course on a more cerebral level than to just blindly follow. You need to be the one to pave your own path. Even if that involves trailing the steps of someone else for a while, never let anyone else hold the map. Every step should be a conscious one, because if you're not careful, your next blind step could lead you right off a cliff!

Again, this is why it is so crucial that you take the time on your journey to pause, reflect and plan ahead.

Whenever I feel at odds with myself, unsure of what my next move should be, I take the time to find some quiet and consider my options, uninterrupted or distracted by anything but my own thoughts. Often, I find just quieting my surroundings and allowing myself to be open to free-flowing thoughts is enough to get my inner voice talking. And then I listen. Good advice that goes ignored is a waste. If you're going to put in the time and energy into synching up with your subconscious, at the very least do it the courtesy of considering whatever it has to offer. You know yourself best, after all. Trust in that.

I've always been something of an extroverted introvert. I love people, and I feed off the positive energy of others. I thoroughly enjoy the experience of being in good company, and I'm in my element when there are others around. At the same time, I know the value of time spent on my own. I've reaped the benefits of alone time often enough to ensure I always get my fix. No one can be "on" all the time, and we all need a little space to regroup here and there. You're not a machine, and if you're not careful, your body will alert you to this in ways you won't like. Get ahead of things and ensure you always carve out a little time for yourself. I'm talking about working with whatever schedule you have, to make a little time when you can, wherever you can. Prioritizing your own peace of mind is always worth it, I promise you. You may not always find yourself with a network of support around you, but you can always count on yourself to keep going—in the best and the worst of times.

I was married for 17 years—and then I wasn't. The emotions behind it may not have been so cut and dry, but the financial aspects were exactly that. I put everything I had into my marriage, and I came out the other side as a single mom starting from scratch. In spite of all the uncertainty, I felt that pull towards a different path. I didn't know what lay ahead, but I knew that taking myself out of park and figuring out what questions to ask had to be the first step towards this next evolution of my life. I didn't want to waste time feeling sorry for myself. I needed to put everything I had into my growth and survival.

This was by no means easy. Emotionally, I was very low. I wasn't sure where the path I was on would take me. At the same time, I knew it wasn't just about me. I had my children to think about, and for them, my time had to be worth more than using it to feel helpless. All of this stress took such a toll on me that I remember one day, completely losing my voice as my throat seized—my body's way of giving me a physical sign that the mental strain was becoming too much. Another day, I awoke feeling like I couldn't move at all, my whole body completely tensed up. I had tested my emotional capacity to its limits, and my body was letting me know that I simply couldn't go on like this.

I had to come to grips with the fact that worrying about things outside of my control wasn't going to get me anywhere. You can't change other people, but you can change your situation. I had to find my breaking point to understand that my first step needed to be forgiveness. I needed to forgive myself for the weight of everything I was carrying on my shoulders, and all the guilt I felt that was weighing me down. I gave myself permission to walk away from the negativity and move forward, to what would be best for my children and me. Sometimes you need to leave it all behind in order to rebuild, and so I did.

It all goes back to defining your purpose. I can't stress enough how critical it is to identify your driving force, to zero in on what it is that makes you tick. That "thing" that inspires you and the overwhelming desire to attain it will be the crutch you lean on in the worst of times. It will be the glue that helps to make your resolve stick.

Consistently having a goal or outcome in mind is your greatest asset on this journey. The more specific, the better. Whether you're thinking in terms of the long haul, or even just your desired outcome for that next phone call you make; setting a clear visual is crucial to taking those next steps towards actualizing what you're after.

One of my favourite rules of survival is to pack your own parachute! Go with your gut, trust in what you know and get educated in what you don't. Do everything in your limitless power from wherever you are in life and always have faith in yourself. Trust that no one has more invested in seeing you find happiness than you.

Keep in mind, your instincts are a guide, not a switch for autopilot; following them does not let you off the hook for doing the work. You're going to get derailed, and your faith is going to be tested, but nothing is more satisfying than working toward something that calls to you from within. I felt that pull in my gut, and every day I've spent headed in that direction has, even on the worst day, been a good day. Beyond success in business and checking off goals, nothing will ever fuel you like the satisfaction of knowing you are living out your authentic life. Find out who you are and what drives you and go from there.

CHAPTER SEVEN

TAKE CONTROL
OF YOUR LIFE!

If you allow people to make more with-
drawals than deposits in your life, you will
be out of balance & in the negative!
Know when to close the account.

—Christie Williams

I could barely see my feet. That's one of the things I remember most vividly when I reflect on my final trimester
with my third child. That, and a brown velour housecoat.
Everyone has their limit, and I remember hitting mine while
tipping the scales—no pun intended—only a few days out
from giving birth.

I knew I would soon find myself in the delivery room, embarking on yet another adventure, the arrival of another
blessing as my first two children had certainly been. I also
knew I would be receiving visitors at the hospital; already a
mother of two, it was a familiar setting. In anticipation of
the birth and the revolving door of well-wishing family and
friends that would follow, I'd had my eye on this brown,

velour housecoat from The Bay. I thought a nice housecoat would be more flattering than the hospital gown alone as we received our loved ones in to see our son for the first time. I mean—I'd earned it! So, one day, I hoisted myself from where I sat and waddled my way into our living room to ask my husband for a housecoat. I reasoned that my birthday was coming up and our son's birth would follow almost immediately after. I guess I figured it would be an appropriate gift.

I realize now that my then-husband simply didn't know better as he responded to my gift-suggestion by reminding me that just a few months earlier, for Christmas, he'd bought me a Filter Queen vacuum. "Wasn't that enough?" he'd asked me. Forget any resentment towards *him*; this moment was all about ME. It felt as though someone suddenly flipped a switch in my mind, and I realized: I AM STANDING HERE, ASKING FOR A HOUSECOAT!

I—the one who'd always worked two jobs and had never had to ask anyone for anything—now stood in front of someone else, asking for a housecoat. *Why was I doing this,* I wondered? *What happened to me?*

When I think back on this story now, I see it as one of those defining moments that acted as a catalyst for a major shift in my perspective. This had nothing to do with my marriage. If anything, at that point in time, with the birth of our third child on the horizon, I was more determined than ever to make the marriage work. I figured if something was broken between us, I could fix it. I wasn't in the business of giving up. No, this had everything to do with me, and the realization that I had somehow forgotten who I was, and who I had authentically been my whole life, up until that period of time. At the end of the day, this was so beyond being about a piece of clothing. *How the hell did I find myself in this position? How had I allowed myself to become someone who felt so small, so inadequate? This wasn't me. Who was this person?*

I began to make some very critical observations about my life as I realized that the shoes in which I stood at that time didn't fit me at all. I needed to get back to being me; I needed to take Vivian out of park! It was a wake-up call to myself. I heard my inner voice speaking up:

Vivian, if you don't like how this feels, CHANGE IT! Change your situation, change the way you're handling it. Just get off your ass and do something! Work on yourself and make a change!!

I thought of the Vivian who took matters in her own hands when she woke up with a face full of acne. That young girl, determined to find her own solutions, where had she gone? Even at that young age, with limited resources, I had exercised my own resourcefulness. I had done what I needed to, and I did so all by myself. With that self-starter in mind, I gave myself a generous helping of tough-love. I felt I'd earned it. Then, I gave myself permission to get back to me.

One of my initial challenges during this time of growth was trying to balance life with a newborn and two young children with the knowledge that I would need to start making some kind of personal income in order to regain that sense of independence. After I gave birth to my third child, I knew I wasn't going to be able to go back to work, so I racked my brain for an alternative solution. Remember, there is ALWAYS another way.

I had heard about the Mary Kay business model through the grapevine and knew that their philosophy was all about a woman's power to balance both a home and work life. It seemed like a viable option for me, so I began working with the beauty brand, selling cosmetics on the weekends. With this job, I earned money for the things I felt I should be able to manage on my own, relieving me of having to ask someone else. In the year I worked with Mary Kay, I reaped not only the benefits of newfound financial independence, but I was also exposed to a network of other ambitious and like-minded women via meetings and company seminars. I was able to maintain my home life while also engaging in a corporate realm that really fed into my desire for personal stability and fulfillment.

I look back now, with the perspective that only 20/20 hindsight can afford, and I fully appreciate the value in the lessons I learned at that time. For each of us, the journey is so different, and our starting points will all vary in monumental ways, but everyone *will* have a moment. When you land on yours, believe me, you'll know.

It all goes back to the concept of taking full responsibility of your life. Otherwise, those pivotal moments will be wasted on you. When you find yourself faced with one of those reality-check experiences, don't throw it away by playing the victim, no matter how hard a pill it is to swallow. The self-indulgent pity party that so many people give in to is a slippery slope. Playing the victim is an addiction for many; it is the easiest role to fall back on when the world deals us cards we don't understand or aren't ready to face. Never fool yourself into believing this is who you are. I've met too many people who relish that feeling of woe-is-me, and

I can tell you, it becomes as real an addiction for them as anything else.

See everything that comes your way as an opportunity for growth and face it head-on. You have everything you need to handle everything life throws at you, and you are more than capable of coming out on the other side as a better person for it. These experiences are life lessons that are instrumental in helping you grow into the person you are meant to be. Don't waste opportunities for greatness just because they come disguised as something else.

Life has this wonderful way of giving us exactly what we need in the very moments in which we have no idea we need it. See your lows as blessings instead. Get motivated—get angry first, if you have to. Just feel something, and then DO something. ANYTHING!

Beyond those very personal "life-altering" moments, you're going to find yourself faced with many challenges in your day-to-day, particularly as it relates to your relationships with others. In these instances, trust yourself enough to let your instincts steer you. At this point, you've come far enough in your journey that you should know your own philosophy of life well enough to help you navigate through. How we communicate and relate to others is a direct reflection of how we view ourselves. Be confident, understand your strengths and respect yourself enough to put boundaries in place to safeguard your own sanity. Believe me, this is easier said than done. It's a process; you must remain focused to see it through.

Relationships, at every level, have the potential to be simple, but we complicate them. Use your own philosophy of life and be conscious when dealing with others; if certain issues keep coming up, then something's got to give. Make the call, make a move, and always be conscientious in your approach.

Prevent issues by staying one step ahead. Understand there's a pulse to every day, something new in the mix, some fresh element or other at play. My business today is not just a single office, and my ability to take the temperature of each day has to be expansive to stay on top of everything that falls within its range.

It's all about relationships in my world, as I play the role of director. Connecting people is a chief part of what I do, as is setting meetings to bring others together. I constantly work to facilitate getting things into motion. My multifaceted industry operates at an international level, and with that comes an international database of clients and realtors. With that in mind, my aim as a director has always been to help guide and move things forward for the benefit of everyone involved. It might seem overwhelming, but with good working habits, and with my personal philosophy and purpose at the forefront of my mind, it really has become second nature.

When you're working towards your purpose, you may grapple with moments of doubt or anxiety, but if you genuinely believe in the course you've laid out for yourself, you will always come back to it. Not everyone starts out with a sense of what their true purpose is; for some that understanding comes later in life. Always remember, this is not a race. This is a journey, and it's your own. So, take all the time you need but start NOW.

When you truly connect with who you are, your whole world will begin to change. It was in those moments where I realized I had forgotten myself that I was best able to hone in on what it was that was missing from my life. From there, I could begin asking the right questions to get me back on track. It's worth repeating that when you zero in on who you are and what your purpose is, a world of opportunity will open up in front of you, allowing you to take control of your own life and the direction in which it's headed.

I meet new people every day, at every level of success and wealth, and I think one of the greatest tragedies of our time is the disillusion that those higher up on the financial rankings are at the top of the charts in happiness, too. While I can't deny that life is obviously made easier by an abundance of wealth, I'm not sure that it has ever singlehandedly made anyone happier. Yes, there are things, experiences and opportunities that wealth can afford to enrich your life, but if you're not nurturing the core desires of your being that lie outside of your bank account, don't expect your level of happiness to change. Money can't buy that.

You can have everything, want for nothing, and still feel empty. That's why I have always encouraged my children, friends, family and colleagues to pursue a life of substance, to live consciously and to give back whenever possible. There are far too many people who struggle with the very real condition of having too little, and I can tell you from experience, nothing will fill your cup more like pouring it out for someone else in need, in whatever capacity you are able to. Always be considerate of others in your personal life as well as in your business life.

Never lose yourself in the trappings of simply chasing that general idea of "success." Instead, be ambitious in your pursuit of living a life of PURPOSE, one that goes beyond simply attaining whatever it is you want in the moment, and doing more with it once it's in your grasp. Set your sights on a life of significance and be relentless in your pursuit of something that holds real value to you. If you find yourself focused only on the idea of acquiring things, your satisfaction will always be short-lived. Only those things with true value can sustain you.

Some people find themselves stagnant in their success and wonder what's missing. The problem is usually rooted in their ultimate driving force; either they've been too short-sighted, or their core purpose wasn't substantial enough to begin with. If you're going to put the best of yourself out there, do so for a greater purpose than a paycheque or a fancy car. Yes, the material lure is very real, and if that's a motivator for you at certain checkpoints on your way, who's to say you're wrong? But at the foundation, beneath all of that, there has to be something more than just the pursuit of a promotion or a higher pay bracket. Those things may come but only when something greater is driving you.

Taking control of your life is about seizing every opportunity and finding your life's purpose in your journey. Ask yourself, What can I learn from this moment? How can this help me to grow? In my experience, it's been the moments of crisis, more than of triumph, that have helped mold me into a better version of myself. I may not have understood it fully at the time, but my efforts to work each moment to my benefit have helped to shape me in ways even I couldn't imagine.

Getting in touch with who you are might surprise you. You might just discover that you don't quite fit in with the crowd as well as you'd hoped. See this as a positive! Use the understanding of everything that makes you unique to help you break from the pack and pave your own way. Don't worry about fitting into a mold or identifying with the expectations others have for you. The greatest strength you have is in working your own unique identity to your benefit. Find what moves you—what really, really moves you! Get behind the wheel and start the engine! Always work from a place of authenticity and you cannot fail.

When I think about the concept of taking control of your life and the struggles we face while trying to simultaneously battle the pressure to fit the mold, I'm reminded of the film, *The Associate*. In it, Whoopi Goldberg plays the part of a businesswoman in an investment firm trying to climb the ranks but consistently loses credit for her work to the men who work above her. Realizing it would be up to her to take the reins on her career, she leaves the firm and starts her own company. Needing an edge against her male competitors, she convinces everyone that she works alongside a male partner, who she calls Robert Cutty. Working on her own but under the veil of this partnership, she begins to see the kind of success she dreamed of when working at her old firm. She soon struggles with living this dual life, as her character goes to extreme lengths to keep the act going before ultimately dropping the façade. In the end, she discovers just what she's made of, and the naysayers discover just how wrong they were to underestimate her.

I've always admired Whoopi's character in this movie. Not for her deception of her colleagues and clients, but for her willingness to find a way to make her mark in an industry that seemed near impossible to break through. Now, more than twenty years since this film was first released, the message still holds: there will always be barriers in place, some structure or other that you just don't fit into—but that doesn't have to be the end of it. Find another way in!

As a woman in a male-dominated industry having experienced firsthand a similar pushback in business, I could relate to Whoopi's character's determination to take control and fight the odds.

After all, when it was first announced I would be buying the corporately owned real estate offices, I knew I would need to come equipped with something to help me in overcoming the criticisms that were sure to follow. By implying I had investors behind me, I was able to assure the people around me that we were solid, giving my agents some added confidence and easing the harsh criticisms coming from my competitors. While the only real investors I had behind me at the time were my bank and me, it was undeniable this strategy worked to ease the skepticisms of those naysayers and to bolster my own confidence long enough to find some solid footing in my new role.

Taking control of your life is about being your own safety net and remaining focused on the path ahead. Don't allow the expectations of others to shake your resolve. Not everyone will be able to see the value you bring to the table, and that's where you'll be forced to either give up or change your approach. Remember: there will *always* be obstacles in your path. Anticipate it, and come prepared to think outside the box.

CHAPTER EIGHT

IT'S NOT YOUR EXPERIENCES THAT DEFINE YOU, IT'S WHAT YOU DO WITH THEM

There is no greater agony than bearing an untold story inside you.

—Maya Angelou

The circumstances and experiences of your life are not what define you. You are not simply a byproduct of everything that has ever happened to you. I say this because, to believe it, would be to believe that *who you are* is solely a result of the things that have happened *to you.*

If this were true, I think most of us would be a real mess. I mean, can you imagine? If the defining elements of who you are came down to the things that had happened *to you,* outside of your control, as opposed to, say, what you've learnt from those experiences?

Simply put, we are not often in the driver's seat of the things that happen *to us*, whereas our resulting reactions and what we do next—how we *evolve* from those experiences—now *that's* 100% in our power! So why then, do we so often find ourselves feeling defined by the things we couldn't prevent, instead of how we handled them?

When I was 18 years old, I was already a world apart from where you might imagine a young person at that age to be. For one, I was married. I was also just stepping into the real estate industry, immediately exposed to the complexities of being a woman in a man's world. I was also unknowingly about to be betrayed by someone I trusted.

This experience would serve as a marker in time, drawing a line between the things I once thought to be true and, after the fact, all the things I couldn't make sense of. It seemed, just as I had found my stride, something unexpected lurked around the corner, something that would violate my mental state and turn my world upside down . . .

I had just started my new career in real estate. I was green to the business world but eager to learn. I felt ready and excited. Already married and knowing children would soon follow, I wanted to establish and grow something for myself while I still had the time to give it as much energy as possible. Fortunately, or so it seemed then, I had a mentor to look to for business advice. He was a successful and prominent figure in the community. As a child, I looked up to him, and as the years passed and my trust grew, I saw this person as a role model, someone I could count on for guidance in my new career. The consummate connector; he had ties throughout the community and beyond—it seemed everyone wanted to get into his elite inner circle.

In a word, he was *magnetic*. All charm and confidence, he walked into a room and everything seemed to gravitate towards him. He was the stereotypical "alpha male." Charismatic, social and well-connected, he was just one of those people you wanted to know. He seemed to always look out for my best interests, and I genuinely trusted him without question. For several years, this larger-than-life "alpha" had become someone I trusted and respected. So it only made sense, when it was time for me to dive into my new career, that this person would volunteer to help me navigate the waters. I felt so fortunate I had a trusted mentor to learn from. I was grateful for this new chapter of my life, and everything seemed to be coming together.

This was also such a departure for me from the parameters of my world leading up to then. Engrained in the traditional and conservative upbringing of a young woman from a Catholic-Italian background, I had attended an all girls' high school, adhered to pretty strict routines and was expressly forbidden to date. I mean—my first boyfriend became my husband—to give you an idea! So that's where I was coming from, and here I was now, 18 years old, a newlywed *and* stepping into the business world.

This was such a happy time for me. I was so thrilled about my new career. This was not only something I would be able to lean on in the future, something I could always hold onto as my own, but this was an industry I was completely fascinated by! My father was in construction as a small builder, so my curiosity in all things related to property had started early on. Every facet of real estate interested me: from matters like land development and property values, to why people moved where and what motivated them—I wanted to learn it all!

Flash forward a few months, and I was beginning to get settled into my new career. One morning, on a day like any other, this mentor, as I had come to see him, asked me to go look at a property with him. This was nothing out of the ordinary, as he'd taken me out to look at properties several times before. I was looking forward to another excursion. Checking out a new development site meant so much more to me than just physically looking at a property. It was another day of learning. It was an opportunity to familiarize myself with new locations, discover where the growth was headed—it was about so much more than a house! I was learning the business, and every day was exciting!

We got into his car and made our way through a busy area toward the property. As we were driving, he pulled over into a local arena to reference his Perly's—for those who might not remember, before GPS, your Perly's directory was *the* go-to for local maps. After a quick flip through his agenda for the address, he set the Perly's down between us on the centre console and turned to the page for the area we were headed. As we both sat there, leaning in towards the map, he suddenly moved in towards my face, getting uncomfortably close. I immediately pulled away and remember thinking, *What the heck?* I felt overcome by total shock. *What just happened?* I looked at him, completely thrown by the situation and said, "Why did you just do that?!"

I was shocked and confused. My mind was reeling. I thought to myself, No. *This did not just happen—could we erase that moment? Can we just wipe it from time?* In my head, I just couldn't process it. *This didn't just happen. There's no way!*

I wanted to hear that this had all been some kind of mistake, some bizarre misunderstanding. I valued our business relationship, and I looked up to him as my mentor; I *trusted* him. This didn't make any sense!

And then suddenly, it seemed, a switch went off for him, as he began to apologize profusely, saying, "Oh my god, I am so sorry! This never should have happened . . ." I remember feeling this wave of relief wash over me, but the confusion still lingered. I really wanted to make sense of the situation. I was glad to hear him express regret, but I still felt sick to my stomach. *This didn't happen*, I told myself. *This was a mistake. He made a mistake. He apologized,* I repeated to myself, *and that's it.*

Not wanting an awkward silence to add to things, I began to talk myself in circles. I was talking a mile a minute, trying to draw some humour out of the situation and somehow bury the incident beneath my words. He had had some kind of breakdown, I reasoned, a momentary lapse in judgment—but he had apologized, hadn't he? I was in uncharted waters here, and all I wanted was to believe that he was truly sorry and go back to how things had been. What other option was there? He immediately took me back to my office, and I went straight back into my usual routine, telling myself that we had left things resolved.

> *When someone shows you who they*
> *are, believe them the first time.*
> —Maya Angelou

A few hours later, I had just sat down with some colleagues in the bullpen room when he came back into the office and said, "Hey Vivian, let's go look at that property."

Behaving completely normally, he seemed to be trying to make amends for earlier by offering to go and look at the site. Feeling as though this would be a good opportunity to bury the hatchet, I accepted. Was I really going to hold a grudge over something that we had both agreed was a mistake?

In considering how quickly he had apologized and acknowledged his error, I felt this was someone I could still trust. By accepting his invitation to go see the property and, in effect, bring the whole event full circle, it was as though we were both getting closure on what he'd done earlier that day.

Like a trooper, I got into his car, and we headed toward the property. Early on in the drive, taking a route I'd travelled many times before, I noticed we'd gotten off the highway before we were meant to. I remember thinking, *Where are we?* Soon after, he made a sharp right turn and pulled onto a dirt road. I immediately began to feel anxious. Not wanting to appear panicked, I took a deep breath and asked him, "Where is this place?" No answer. Another sharp right turn. Now we were off the dirt road and headed into a wooded area. Something wasn't right.

I asked him again, "Where is this place?" But he just kept driving, and that's when I noticed his face had completely changed. It was as though the person I knew had transformed before my eyes. At that point, there was no use denying it—I was petrified. As the car slowed, I reached for the door handle but realized the passenger door had been electronically locked from the master lock on the driver's side. I had no way of knowing what was going on, but I knew from the look on his face that something was very, very wrong.

Suddenly, he stopped the car and shut off the engine. Without saying a word, he lunged. This was nothing like earlier that day. This was not some kind of a "come-on"— this was aggressive, angry and violent—this was someone else entirely. I was frightened for what he might do. I knew in my gut this was not headed to a good place. He seemed motivated by anger as I struggled to protect myself, pleading with him to stop. In trying to get him to back off, I was saying anything I could think of that I thought might resonate with him in some way, desperately trying to diffuse the situation.

I told him, "Stop, please, I'm sorry! This is my fault!!"

I needed him to snap out of it, to get off of whatever crazy track he was on. It seemed to work, as he suddenly stopped and moved away from me, slumping back into his seat. I looked over at him and saw tears streaming down his cheeks, his face still contorted in rage, his hands balled into fists. I was terrified. The muddled emotions he seemed to be going through, the hostile behaviour . . . I didn't know this person. *Who was this person? What would he do next? Dear lord*, I silently prayed, *help me. What do I do?*

He had become a stranger in that moment, someone totally unpredictable. I had no idea what might come next, and not wanting to draw attention to myself, I sat still in my seat, lowering my head, cowering in an almost subservient way in the hope he would calm down and just stop whatever this was.

His reaction was the opposite. As he turned to me, he began shouting, "You're right, this is all your fault!" He then proceeded to call me every name in the book. Every terrible thing he called me, he had me recite back to him, as though in repeating his words, I would be acknowledging them as the truth. At this point, as long as he was physically not hurting me, I was resigned to saying whatever I needed to in order to pacify him.

I remembered that my door had been electronically locked from his side, and now that the engine was off, I thought to try it again. I slid my hand toward the lock and found it, now able to unlock my door. The desperation I felt when I hurtled myself out of that car and away from him is something I can hardly describe. I bolted as he called back after me. I ran through the bush and back onto the paved highway we had turned off of. He followed me with his car and demanded I get in, but I refused. Standing there, at the roadside of this busy highway, I flagged down a passing truck. I can't imagine what I must have looked like as I clambered into the passenger seat of this stranger's truck and recited the address to my office while looking down at my hands folded on my lap. I remember the man asking me, "Miss, are you all right?"

"I don't know . . ." I stammered. "No, I'm not all right."

Once I got to my office, I immediately got into my car. I knew, of course, in the state I was in, I couldn't go home. At the time, my husband and I were temporarily living with my parents, and in that moment, the thought of facing everyone just wasn't an option. So instead, I headed toward the home of a colleague and friend. I hadn't been there more than five minutes before there was a knock at her door. My friend excused herself, and I felt my stomach turn over as I heard her open the door, and I heard his voice reply to her greeting. As he, my friend and her husband were all well acquainted, nothing seemed odd to her about him swinging by to say hello. Mindful of his tone, he asked to speak with me. "Just a quick chat with Vivian, do you mind?" When she invited him in, he politely refused, saying he was in a rush, and could she please ask me to come to the door for a quick second?

In a zombie-like state, I walked over to the entryway, where I saw him standing behind the screen door. I stayed on my side of the screen—this was close enough.

In a soft but firm voice, he leaned in to the screen door and said, "Nobody's going to believe you. It's your word against mine." And with that, he smiled and called out a goodbye to my friend, who hurried to the door to wave him off.

Once he left, I sat down at her kitchen table, my face buried in my hands, as she asked, "What's wrong?"

Trying to put it into words, I realized I just didn't know what to say. How could I explain what had happened when even I didn't understand it? Worse, how could I possibly relive the moment? What could I say? Worst still, my friend and her husband both respected and admired this person. He was right; no one would ever believe me. It would be my word against his.

From that day forward, whenever our paths crossed, it was as though he had completely wiped the incident from his memory. He acted as if nothing happened. But for me, it was a painful struggle to move forward, still carrying the trauma of the events of that day with me. Over time, I learned how to avoid him to some degree, but I would still have to see him at certain business engagements and industry events. Every time I saw him, I would feel that same sick and twisted knot in the pit of my stomach.

You would think that after what had happened, he would avoid me too. Instead, he took every opportunity (always in front of an audience) to go out of his way to do "nice" things for me. He knowingly put me in the position of having to be civil in response to his overblown gestures and "friendly" disposition. It was as if his cruelty knew no bounds.

Something inside of me felt completely broken. Would I ever be able to trust anyone again? Even as time passed, I continued to feel a lingering sense of self-doubt casting a shadow over each step I took. I kept asking myself, *What did I do wrong?* From where I stood, my only "mistake" had been to ever trust him and view him as a mentor.

Even though in my heart, I knew none of what had happened had been my fault, I still couldn't make peace with it. *Is this what happens when you trust somebody?* I wondered. Memories would flash through my mind of everything that had come before, all those "little moments" that had come together to create the foundation of trust that I thought was real. Now it all seemed tainted—as though none of it had been sincere. I knew I wasn't to blame for his actions and for what happened that day, but I certainly played a part in everything that had come after. In allowing the experience to hold such weight in my mind, I actively carried those negative feelings with me, like bricks, for years after the fact.

Looking back, I can still feel the overwhelming shock and betrayal that my 18-year-old self felt when I discovered just how deeply people could hurt you. It's not that the experience rendered me incapable of trusting others; on the contrary, the pain it caused me, and the darkness it brought to my life, enabled me to become a stronger person. Unfortunately, it would be a long time before I would be able to recognize and engage that inner strength.

There are no guarantees when you put your trust in others, and while it's always worth the risk to establish bonds, whatever the context, you have to be prepared for the occasional fallout. And though my experience in this case was in a more extreme sense, the point remains: sometimes the people you least expect can and will disappoint you. This is just a fact. One of the key takeaways for me was the understanding that, even if it didn't feel like it, I was the only one in control of my own life. And I refused to feel sorry for myself. While I no doubt went through a rollercoaster of emotions during this time, self-pity wasn't one of them. Had I let myself become consumed with self-pity, I have no doubt it would have drowned me. And while I indulged in my own self-destructive behaviours after the fact, I never—ever—felt sorry for myself. To do that would have robbed me of whatever inner strength I had left. No, of everything I was feeling, I definitely wasn't feeling that. I had choices—and though it took me some time, I ultimately chose to move forward.

I had spiraled out slowly but steadily in the aftermath of that day. My world had been turned inside out in one afternoon, and I had no choice but to deal with it on my own. In trying to numb and somehow cope with the feelings that kept rising up, I found myself making the wrong decisions and turning to self-destructive behaviours, hoping those things would help to bury the ones I couldn't forget. I was projecting out and onto myself all of the hurt and anxiety that brewed within.

I felt boxed in with my emotions, unable to let them out into the open, but also incapable of detaching myself from them entirely. The events of that day had wreaked havoc on my self-confidence as I had been made to believe I was worthless. I felt ashamed, as though I were guilty of something—and very much alone.

I had flashbacks of when I was made to call myself all kinds of names—none worth repeating—and even long after the fact, I could still hear the echo of my own voice, reciting those terrible things aloud. It had been one of the lowest points of my life, to endure something so degrading and dehumanizing—I felt powerless. It was as though that day had robbed me of something I couldn't quite define. The inner strength I needed to move forward was buried deep inside of me, but at the time, it felt so out of reach. Even with so many people around me, I still felt completely alone.

Some years after the fact, shortly after my divorce and very much during a dark time for me, I received a phone call I will never forget. It was a familiar voice on the other end of the line—one that wouldn't wait to hear me speak more than a few words before saying flatly, "You're a disgrace to the community. Why don't you put a gun to your head and pull the trigger?"

Can you imagine being on the receiving end of something like that? This call was a crushing blow to me. I might never know exactly what had prompted this call, but it wasn't hard to guess the intention: this person, clearly unhappy with my choices, was trying to keep me in a box and remind me of "my place"—as he saw it, anyways. I had stepped off the course of his expectations with my decisions, and in doing so, had gone against our customs and become the black sheep. I was now a divorced woman from a traditional Catholic background—I knew there would be backlash from others—but my priority was being honest with myself and doing right by my children, who didn't deserve to suffer from any of this—they had to be my focus.

Still, this person's words had left me feeling completely depleted of my will to fight. I won't lie to you; I gave some real thought to what he had said as I sat there, internalizing his every word, repeating it over and over in my head. But then my children's faces came to mind—and I thought of them, the most important people in my life. I considered, *Will my children be okay without me?*

The answer, of course, was clear. It was about more than me. I found strength in something greater than myself—the love of my kids. Here were these three beautiful, innocent children—of everything I had done in my life up to that point, I had certainly done this part right. My love for them would be the beacon of light I needed to help guide me through the dark.

In your bleakest of moments, ones like these, where you begin to believe the worst about yourself, remember that there is always something greater to look to for strength. Every breath you take is a testament to the fact that you are strong and capable and worth every bit of love and support as anyone else. Never let anyone rob you of that, not even for a moment.

In the moments after I got that call, in need of some inspiration to trigger my own inner strength, my thoughts went to my grandmother. She was one of the strongest women I have ever known. She was a mother to nine children: two of which she would lose tragically during the war, and seven of which she would raise on her own for several years while my grandfather himself was away at war. By the time my grandparents joined the rest of our family in Canada, four of their children were already married, and so it would be the two of them and their two remaining children, teenagers, who would join my family at my aunt and uncle's house, where we were all staying at the time. I have fond, albeit brief, memories of my grandfather, who would ultimately choose to return to Italy within his first year in Canada. You can imagine the shock from our family when my grandmother refused to return with him! Looking back, it's not hard to see why my Nonna Rosa carried the reputation for being such a tough woman, and unfortunately, one who many in our family viewed then as a disgrace to the community.

Nonna Rosa used to babysit my cousin and me when our parents went off to work. In our eyes, she was the kind of grandmother you feared, and one whose reputation painted her as anything but traditional. As children, we would hear our uncles talk of how she shamed the family by not staying by her husband's side and supporting his decision to move back to Italy. She had made a decision that had shocked our family and gone against the ideals of what it meant to be a "good wife." Still, she stood her ground and never backed down from the choices she had made. Ignoring the whispers of those around her and within our tight-knit community, she defied the critics by keeping her head up and never wavering in her resolve.

Over the years, I was amazed to see the shift in reception my nonna would get as the men of the community went from looking down on her to genuinely respecting her. I remember watching the men in our busy neighborhood pass her home, always taking a moment to tip their hat at my nonna as they walked by.

As I got older, I became closer with my nonna. She would tell me stories of her past, and my admiration for her continued to grow. There was one conversation in particular that stuck with me, as she sat down with me one day and imparted some wisdom that I would never forget. She said, "As you grow, be true to yourself when making decisions. Don't do things just to make other people happy. Never give in to criticism, and don't ever let anyone hold you back." And, in a final thought, she sighed before saying, "If I could do it all over again . . . what I could have done with my life!" This was as powerful to me then as it continued to be in some of the darkest moments of my life. This strong and resilient woman never let the ridicule and judgment of others cloud her convictions. It would be her spirit that I would channel in moments where I felt the most powerless and alone.

During the darkest time of my life, I found I struggled the most with feelings of loneliness. I was carrying this "secret" around with me like a bag of bricks, and it was weighing me down more and more. Looking into the mirror, I didn't recognize myself. Who was this person? I felt marked. I had been tricked, preyed on and demeaned in a way I could never have imagined. I wondered how long these feelings would last?

I've discovered that predators count on this. They rely on the lasting effects of their actions: the fear you feel in speaking up, the crushing loneliness at not being able to confide in family or friends, the shame and guilt that defies logic but exists anyways.

While I believe this self-destructive point of my life was the result of a combination of factors, there's no doubt in my mind that those unaddressed feelings were often the trigger for whatever spiral would come after. A pattern of regression and rebellion developed; and my indifference to these behaviours only further handicapped my ability to heal. I was suffering from a real lack of self-confidence, struggling to harness my own inner strength. And while I've always believed that only I could be held accountable for my life, I had trouble pushing aside the toxic thoughts that had been embedded in my mind long enough to get back into my stride. It felt as though I just couldn't grasp the reins and take back control. Instead of growing into a complete person, I had been fractured by that day and left wondering how and when I might ever heal.

People who hurt you in this way don't deserve to occupy this much room in your head. They don't warrant the energy. This is much, *much* easier said than done, obviously. But take it from someone who carried that bag of bricks for far longer than I should have: these people just aren't worth it.

There was a significant stretch of time in my life when, while I continued to function, I was living a semi-hollow life. And as the time passed and everything around me seemed to reset, I still felt as though I was stuck in that moment with lead feet. I knew I needed to get past this—or at the very least, find a way to heal.

When everything had happened, not speaking up had been a very personal decision. While I know it may be hard to understand, at that moment, what I needed most was to focus on my own strength. I needed to respect myself enough to reflect on my own power and how *I* would take back control of *my* life. I needed to look in the mirror and see a reflection of myself I could be proud of. I was a good person, a good daughter, and I was a good mother. I was a hard worker, and I was strong. None of that was anyone's doing but my own, and I refused to give the thought of that day another minute in my mind. It didn't happen overnight but, eventually, my self-confidence began to grow, and I felt as though I had finally turned the page on that chapter of my life. Once again, I was confident and hopeful for the future.

Flash-forward 40 years to present-day and I am walking into a business event, looking forward to enjoying some time with my colleagues. You can imagine my surprise when one of the first familiar faces I see is his. I suppose I shouldn't have been that shocked to see him. Though our paths don't cross often anymore, they do still intersect on occasion. I readied myself for the usual exaggerated greeting and nauseating pleasantries I had come to expect from him. But this time it was different. In fact, was it my imagination or was this person *avoiding me*? Before long, we were again (nearly) face to face as someone I had been chatting with spotted him and tapped him on the shoulder to turn around. Now there was no question in my mind—he was absolutely avoiding me! I had to stop myself from laughing out loud—this person, this *coward*, was AFRAID OF ME!

I was joyful, to say the least! For once, it was *ME* he didn't want to see! Finally, it was his turn to do the avoiding! He quickly excused himself, leaving the person next to me completely puzzled at the interaction. This wasn't like him. This was someone who usually thrived on the opportunity to puff out his chest and make a scene—this was someone who never blinked first or missed an opportunity to put on the charm. What had changed?

And then it dawned on me. His obvious refusal to engage or risk confrontation—this was someone who had clearly been keeping up to date with the current headlines. At the moment, the news is overflowing with allegations of misconduct, accusations of assault, and victims who are finally being heard. The current has shifted, and it's a new day! I will say, in my resilience in finding a positive place beyond that experience, I feel very much apart – and proud - of this wave of change.

Coming full circle to this whole experience, something I want to make sure I get across, is a message for any of you who can relate to my story in some way: you are loved, and you are not alone—and most importantly, everything you need is already within you.

I know from my own experience that the true healing begins with you. Everything I needed to move forward had to come from within, and that meant facing my demons and making peace with the past. While I wasn't able to grasp this at the time, it's something that gives me a lot of peace now, because I know that someone out there will read this and see themselves in my story somehow, and feel the sincerity of my words and my journey.

When I consider the current state of things as it relates to those who have been victims of intimidation, harassment or assault, I feel optimistic for the future. Though I'm sure we can all agree that, in 2018, it's a bit disappointing to have to revisit conversations we had hoped were no longer necessary, it's a testament to our strength in numbers that both women and men have come together to take a stand in such a big way. Everyone deserves to be respected and heard. Never forget: your voice matters, and YOU are in control of your own life.

CHAPTER NINE

MY "AHA" MOMENT WITH OPRAH

Think like a queen. A queen is not afraid to fail.
Failure is another steppingstone to greatness.
—Oprah Winfrey

One of the most impactful lessons of my life, both professionally and personally, has been to find and understand the value in my failures. By choosing to interpret the missteps of my life as steppingstones towards something greater, I have learned to better translate criticisms and further support my own self-confidence. My personal struggles have been the greatest catalysts for self-validation on my journey, as they have given me the chance to discover my own strength and resilience firsthand. To that end, leadership requires more than just self-confidence; the real skill is in knowing when to look inward, and when to look out. You may not always welcome the communications coming your way, but learning to interpret and unearth the value in them will only strengthen your leadership skills.

When we talk about criticism, the first feelings that spring to mind for most of us are those of anxiety and insecurity. Our minds have been programmed to relate the idea of criticisms as being negative indicators, red flags designed to alert us to our failings. But this just isn't the case. As with everything else, criticism is simply another language for us to interpret and process in a constructive way. This means that the value—or lack of value—which we take from communications of this nature is entirely up to us.

When I made the decision to buy my brokerage, I was met with anything but high-fives and congratulatory gift baskets. The naysayers said I couldn't do it. The general consensus amongst those who doubted me was that in an industry that was as much of a boys' club as real estate was at the time, I just didn't fit the mold.

I heard it all. There were no shortages of people betting on me to fail, and some days, it felt like I was the only one in my corner. But as I've said, it's in those moments when your back is to the wall that you find out what you're really made of. I had made up my mind, I was focused on the task at hand—and even if I was only a cheering squad of one, I liked my odds. I may not have fit the traditional vision of what an industry leader looked like at the time, but so what? Wasn't change, doing something different and breaking from the status quo what progress was all about? I knew if I was ever going to make a difference and have a *real impact*, it wasn't going to be by blending in! To take on this new role as a leader, I would have to learn to decipher the languages of my business and managing criticism would be an integral part of that.

It's not surprising that the first association that comes to mind for most people when you broach the subject of criticism is the "bad stuff"—the negativity of the naysayer, the sharp-tongued jerk or simply the bully who defies logic or reason. So, let's start there. When my kids were young and would come home with stories about bullies in the schoolyard, I always offered them the same advice. I told them that people who look to hurt others for no reason are just masking their own pains; it says everything about how unhappy they are with themselves and often has nothing to do with their target. You're just a casualty of convenience, I would tell them. You can't help the actions of others, but you do have FULL CONTROL over your own reactions. If you refuse to give people the reactions they seek, you strip them of their power.

It's a sad reality that for as long as there have been good and decent people looking to better their situations, there have been those who seemingly exist only to knock them down. It's unfortunate to think we haven't risen above a culture of trying to heal our own scars by inflicting fresh ones on others, but that's just the way it is for some. Criticism has many forms and faces, but the one that will baffle you the most will be the bully.

This is why focus is so essential. Never give anyone the power to veer you off course—particularly not those who come at you with baseless judgments and ulterior motives. No one like that is worth a kink in your chain. Choose to rise above it, and consider yourself fortunate to be of so much importance that someone else has dedicated so much energy to making their way into your orbit. Fans come in all forms, after all. Thick skin and a mature perspective are all you need to combat this. You're not in the schoolyard anymore, and people can only make you feel whatever way you allow them to.

Be realistic about the world you live in. Not everyone around you has the best intentions, and unfortunately there will be no shortage of those who wish to break you down. Anticipate this as you navigate your way toward your goals, and do your best to always handle these types of hurdles with humility and grace. How someone approaches you speaks to their character, how you respond speaks to yours.

Now that we've covered the less constructive end of the criticism spectrum, let's get back to focusing on the positive.

Not every ounce of criticism you encounter will be at the hands of a bully, and it would be a true disservice to yourself to write it all off as such. You need to start looking at criticism in a new way. Where many people may see it as a barrier, I see it as an integral component of progress. Consider adulthood as your master class in the field of redefining how you interpret criticism, because there's no doubt those experiences will play an essential role in both your personal and professional growth.

In my work life, I make a point of surrounding myself with people who have the miles, who are experienced in what they do and have something valuable to contribute. I never operate under the assumption that everyone is going to agree with me all the time, nor do I hope for it. In fact, if everyone at the table is nodding in agreement at every meeting, it's a clear indicator that something is very wrong.

People just aren't designed to blindly follow without opinion. Following the herd is a learned behaviour and not one I encourage, unless of course you can be sure of where you're being led! When I sit down with my team, I urge them to communicate beyond the basics. I want to create a dialogue where we are all engaged and feel acknowledged—whether we agree with each other's opinions and ideas or not.

It's that constructive banter that really gets the juices going, amps up the conversation and often leads us somewhere great, somewhere outside of the box!

Without embracing feedback or considering opposing views, you can never aim to reach those at the higher levels; at this tier of business, it takes more than just one independent train of thought to stay ahead as innovators in the industry.

I immerse my team and myself in these think-tank situations at every opportunity. This give-and-take is the only way I know how to lead. This is where I can strengthen the bonds and enhance the communication between my team and me. These discussions stir up new ideas, contrasting opinions and a constructive dialogue on what to do next. I can then filter through these ideas, forming them into an end result that my team can feel they are a part of. Ultimately, it's on me to make the final call, and that's a responsibility in leadership that I embrace wholeheartedly.

When you work toward the greater good for your team at every step, you'll find peace of mind knowing you've taken a proactive route towards establishing an even-handed foundation on which to make decisions.

In both my personal and business life, I have always felt the biggest sign of mutual respect is open dialogue—fair and honest communication. You simply cannot equate fear with respect. It may seem an unorthodox approach, but when my kids were growing up, I didn't discourage them from criticizing me when they felt something was unfair. I went the other way instead.

I would tell them, "Go ahead. Tell me why you think I'm wrong. Plead your case; you have the floor. Speak your mind!" Truth be told, I've got some clever kids. More often than not, they communicated in such a way that they left me reconsidering my position, if not agreeing to some compromise or another. I have always seen this as progressive. Being a leader, or representing some figure of authority in your world, should never be managed as a dictatorship, and you shouldn't expect to work towards positive resolutions unless you've heard from everyone on board. Everyone's opinion has value, and even if it's not something you necessarily *want* to hear, it may turn out to be something you *need* to hear. It's worth repeating that criticism, at its core, is really just a language needing to be interpreted. What you translate and take away from it is up to you.

For your part, try not to look at criticisms as "What am I doing wrong?" but instead see it from the perspective of "How can I—or we—do better?"

In every situation, I try to examine things from a constructive angle. I consider, "How can we improve? How can we make this more effective or more efficient? What new channels can we explore?" This is where the value of collective input really comes into play.

It boils down to this: you never want the people around you to feel as though they have no voice or that their opinion doesn't matter just because it doesn't align with your own.

To this same point, know the value in your own opinions and be confident in speaking up. Even a broken clock is right twice a day, so never doubt yourself. If you're in the right company, they will be as happy to hear you out, as you are to hear them. Communication is a give and take, and by setting the example in your own methods, you also establish an expectation in respect and fair dialogue that works to everyone's benefit.

In my position, I try to always work from a place of mindfulness when dealing with others. After all, you never really know what it is to walk in someone else's shoes. Be the kind of colleague or leader you would like to work for. Emulate the behaviour and receptive nature of someone you enjoyed working for in the past, or someone you admire who carries those traits. It isn't always second nature to feel out the best response to new scenarios, but it helps to have someone in mind whom we can reflect on, whose actions and attitude we respect—until we can find a level of comfort and confidence in our own methods. Reflecting on the actions and philosophies of people you admire will work to inspire you in your own strategies going forward.

As children, we look to our parents and other authority figures to fashion our own behaviours. As adults, we look to those we see as mentors to help us in our more "grown-up" ambitions. Not everyone will aspire to seek out a mentor, but be sure to dedicate some time to reading up on the success stories of those in similar industries. Reflect on the journeys of people you admire and respect, and seek out new ways to get inspired, surrounding yourself with people who contribute to your life in a positive way.

I have always felt a great significance in doing things my own way, but I would never discount the lasting—and sometimes life-changing—impact that's come from tuning in to the experiences of others. Fortunately for me, I have been blessed in this regard, having had some rare opportunities to witness firsthand the power of sourcing inspiration from some of the truly great figures of our time.

In 2012, I was part of a committee that was working to bring Oprah Winfrey to Toronto. At this time, Oprah was scheduled to speak at the Peabody Opera House in St. Louis as part of her Life Class Tour. When I was invited to go, it was a no-brainer. Oprah has always been something of an idol of mine, this flesh and blood actualization of overcoming obstacles and reaching your highest potential. Would I pass up the opportunity to see this person speak live? No way!

I remember the lineup outside the venue. It was endless! A sea of people waiting to see Oprah, all eager just to be in her presence. From her perspective, I wondered if she's ever gotten used to this rock star reception and the multitudes of people who would buy a ticket at any cost and fly anywhere just to hear her speak . . .

As we got closer to the start of the show, I was granted back-stage access. This was where I would get my first glimpse of Oprah as she and her crew were ushered into the area where I was seated with others. She walked in wearing flip-flops, smiling and stopping to speak with everyone she passed. At the front and centre of her entourage was her makeup artist, of whom she raved about their 25-year relationship working together. Her energy was infectious, and I was surprised to see her looking not only excited, but also nervous!

When it was time for her to go out on stage, I watched as she went into her routine and readied for the moment. Putting her hand on her makeup artist's shoulder, she slipped into these spectacular (and sky-high!) shoes he had set out for her and glided out onto the stage. The roar of the crowd was deafening—Oprah was ready!

In true form, Oprah started off with gratitude, expressing how happy she was to be there and how she'd truly missed being in front of an audience. This was in 2012, a time when Oprah was coming off of some harsh criticisms of her OWN network. Seizing the opportunity to get candid with her fans, Oprah spoke openly about what she was going through with the network, explaining that some of the challenges she now faced were, in part, a credit to her having taken the advice of others. Now, she went on, she was doing her best to work her way out of a bad situation and, as she'd so often advised others, looking to see the experience as a teaching moment.

At the end of the show, Oprah returned to our section backstage and immediately kicked off her heels, scooping them up into her hands as she asked us, in a serious tone, "So how did I do?"

I was floored. Oprah was asking us *how she did?* This was Oprah—queen of network television, international icon for so many, not to mention a major source of inspiration in my own life—and here she stood, asking this room of strangers for validation. This woman is more than just a talk-show host—she's a *universal brand*, a life coach, a teacher, a motivator, and a very spiritual being. She is someone who represents so many things to so many people, and here she was looking to us for input. Imagine!

This was such a surreal moment for me. For one thing, I felt totally empowered by Oprah's energy. It was such a rush just to be standing in the presence of someone whom I'd admired for so long—and at the same time, incredibly inspiring. Oprah's humble nature had been unexpected, and it truly was one of those signature "teaching moments" for me as I listened to her openly discuss her own mistakes and actively seek out constructive criticism from others in a bid to improve her situation. Now this was someone who spoke the language of criticism fluently! This was someone who understood the value in owning your mistakes!

At my own lowest point, I ultimately realized that my greatest source of validation had to come from within. It was seeing those lows and owning my mistakes that helped me become stronger. While it had taken a new perspective on criticism to help get me there, I had to first discover the power of trusting and validating myself in place of looking to others for assurances. As Oprah spoke about her struggles in coping with the harsh lessons of the past year, I reflected on my own low points, and just what it took for me to bring myself out of the darkness and back into the light.

It must have been as humbling for Oprah as it was illuminating for me to hear her speak so candidly about her own missteps. I found myself thinking, *"I guess it wasn't just me after all!"*

It's interesting that when you find yourself at the centre of your own storm, it really can feel as though you're the only one, but that's just not the case. This experience was proof-positive that anyone, at any level, can make mistakes and find their way back onto higher ground. The newspapers had been reeling for months surrounding Oprah's issues with the new network, and I recall one headline in particular reading, "Oprah's OWN Financial Flop!" That's gotta hurt! And yet, here she was, front and centre of her fans and critics alike, bouncing back with grace, humility, and optimism for the future.

One thing was crystal clear: for Oprah, the adversity of the past year had only strengthened her resolve. Twenty-five years of experience had equipped her with the ability to not only relish in her successes, but to also confront any hurdle and come out fighting on the other side. If I'd ever wondered what aspect of this woman's character I hoped to adopt as my own, there was no question now. She was a fighter, and a survivor, through and through.

I saw in Oprah a familiar determination and sense of spirituality, someone who had faced crisis and felt the gut-wrenching lows, while struggling to regain her footing, as I had also done. And now here she stood, reaching out to the people around her for feedback, understanding that owning your mistakes and re-working them in a positive way is the key to creating something good from something that usually feels anything but.

Not surprisingly, the event and the experiences of that day were hugely significant for me. The greatest lesson I took away from this experience was that of validation. Having the strength to own your mistakes and resurface with confidence in yourself is something that you simply cannot teach. This is an aspect of character that comes from experience—period. Mistakes are inevitable, but it's from here that real personal growth happens. Self-confidence will allow you the maturity to look outward for criticisms when needed but, more importantly, the self-assuredness to look inward for the validation that only you can give.

In opening myself up to the opportunity of seeing this inspirational person speak, I had opened up the doors for so much greatness—all because I had been willing to listen to the guidance of someone who was looking to share from her own experiences. There was no magical element at play, it was simple logic; if I were open to it, the power of positive thinking and a proactive approach to every opportunity would prevail. From this, I have never forgotten the power of being open to the ideas and wisdom of others, nor have I let the opportunity slip to share what I can with those who might benefit from it, as I have.

It really all comes back to the idea of criticism and the understanding that this, too, is simply another language to translate, another opportunity for growth and progression. Your perspective will make all the difference as you engage with others to either meet dead-ends or break barriers and create new opportunities.

At the end of the day, good or bad, I want to hear it all. There is enormous value to being in touch with the opinions of others. Not only does it help to keep you grounded, it also allows you to gain perspective on how others view you and the work you're doing. It can be so difficult to truly get outside of our own heads long enough to form an objective opinion on how we are doing—at work, in our parenting, in our relationships, all of it. Opening up to the insights of others can be so refreshing, and inspiring! What others bring to the conversation is up to them; how you react and what you make of it is up to you.

CHAPTER TEN

LEARN FROM YOUR MISTAKES

Do not be embarrassed by your fail-
ures, learn from them and start again.
—**Richard Branson**

The most successful people in business are not where they are today because they've mastered the art of succeeding by sheer "luck." Rather, they find themselves in the top percentile of their industries because they've become masters at learning from their early failures, which paved the way to their successes. These people see their mistakes as opportunities to get it right. They dust themselves off and get back up and try again, armed with the insight of one way it won't work, and all the more equipped to find ways in which it will.

Most people find the idea of analyzing their mistakes daunt-ing, and I can certainly understand the appeal of wanting to brush your mistakes under the rug and move forward. After all, so much of this is a nod to our upbringing—our efforts to fit the mold, the idea that it's embarrassing to come up short or that it might be shameful to make mistakes, to not "get it right" on our first, second or third try—where our early "failures" are seemingly an indicator that we are not capable. Well let me tell you, this just isn't true! The top people in their field know better. You need to recognize the tremendous value in retracing your steps and zeroing in on the reasons you weren't successful in your attempts. Only then can you uncover the path to get it right the next time. Get over this idea of failing as "weak," and while we're at it, let's grow beyond the idea of equating mistakes with failure—there's just no truth to that.

Retrain your brain to see your mistakes as steppingstones on your path to success. Every time you get it wrong just means you are one step closer to getting it right. Each step is different and necessary; some are easier to land on than others, but all are critical to getting you from where you are to where you want to be.

Stumbling is a part of growth and achievement. If getting what you want was easy, everyone would do it. But you're not looking for an easy life, you're looking for a GREAT one, and that takes work. It takes trial and error. It takes falling on your ass, getting back up and going again, and again, until you've exhausted every angle. That's where you succeed. That persistence and grit is going to take you further than anything else. And believe me, you'll want to leave your ego at the door.

While the process of elimination leads you towards knowing what to do, learning what *not* to do is also very important. Your missteps are there to help guide you! You have to believe this. Say it out loud, make it part of your daily mantra, do whatever it takes to embed into your mind that "mistakes" are a critical part of the process. These "wrong" paths will only help you to discover the right one. Never be so shortsighted as to think that these lessons are one-shot deals. No way! All of these lessons are going to stay with you on your journey. Remember when we talked about our instincts and the way in which we add to them with our experiences?

This is a BIG part of that!

The lessons you learn now are not only going to help you with your current ventures, but will also internalize themselves and become part of the fabric of your instincts. These are the experiences that will come to surface in later challenges and conflicts, helping to guide you onto the right path. Your mistakes may be short-lived in the moment, but if you handle them with care, they're sure to serve you well in the future. Learning from your past and consciously moving forward with those lessons in tow is all a part of good work habits.

As a young girl, I witnessed the great pains my parents took to provide us with the best life possible: giving us all the opportunities they never had, for our benefit and for our future. It takes getting outside of your comfort zone to make something of yourself in this world.

Even in my adolescence, I understood that in a world full of people who are out for the same thing, you have to rely on a strong will above all else if you want to stand out. With little education, language barriers and no money, moving to the Western world was a choice my parents had made based on their own strong will and determination to stay focused and use their good work habits to make it work, somehow, for our family's sake. Their ensuing challenges would all serve as springboards on their path to getting it right.

The reality is there will always be someone who is smarter, stronger or faster just waiting for their turn behind you. Someone out there has it in spades, and someone behind them has more than that. Stop looking outward. Instead, get used to looking inward. Only you can make it happen. Never be complacent about your life. The moment you do, you risk backsliding and undoing the work you've put in. Sometimes, in spite of your best efforts, you may still find you come up short. So what? Don't dwell on it—learn from it! Simply doing your best may not always be enough, but that's okay. Sometimes, it's those moments in which you fall short that you are led toward your greatest opportunities.

See your "failures" as getting one step closer to being better and coming back stronger than before. Understand that hard work is a constant, not just a means to an end. To get to where you want to be, you're going to have to put in the hours, day after day. Be ready to commit wholeheartedly to what you want, and be willing to work for it.

Ready—set—GO!

If you aren't prepared or willing to do the work, there's just no way you can succeed. When people ask me what the secret to my success is, I ask them, "What secret?!"

Personal success comes from knowing at your core that you're working toward something that fuels your purpose. It's remaining *focused*. For me, it's getting up every day committed to my goals and looking forward to doing everything I can to get it right and help others. It's about putting forth my best effort not just for myself, but also for the people who depend on me to set the example. My *job*? It's a way of life for me; it's my way of *living*!

In some form or another, I've been working since I was 12 years old. From that time, I began building my experiences, growing and fine-tuning my work ethic, always eager to do my best and learn from those around me. It was in those early years working at the snack bar that I recall learning one of my first critical lessons in business: always be PREPARED.

It was in my first job working at the popcorn stand that I began juggling roles between there and the connected snack bar, always under the watchful eye of my manager, Mary Purvis. She would be one of the earliest female figures to make an impact in my life. She was tough, frugal and taught me so much about hard work and multitasking. I did everything. From taking orders to flipping burgers to taking out the trash—there was no task that lay outside my job description.

One evening, after a particularly long shift at the popcorn stand, I had just finished carting some heavy, soiled bags of garbage out back and was due to start on the snack bar side when my manager came out to meet me.

There I stood, the last bag of stinking garbage slung low at my side, as she proceeded to give me a once-over. I was filthy. My white apron was stained and wrinkled, an occupational hazard from bagging buttered popcorn all day for customers.

With a raised brow, she told me, "You can't go back in there and serve food at the snack bar like that. Didn't you bring a change of clothes and another clean apron? Didn't you come prepared?"

Was I prepared? I'd certainly thought so. I'd come in a full fifteen minutes before my shift. I'd tied my hair back, worn the right shoes, and ensured my skirt was an appropriate length for work. But after taking a moment to consider the situation from my manager's perspective, I realized that none of the above would compensate for the fact that I hadn't considered bringing a change of clothes, so I shook my head: *no.*

Saying nothing, my manager took me into the back room where she produced a clean apron for me to change into. This was a teaching moment. Even with the expectation that her employees should be prepared, she herself had further prepared in case we hadn't. It dawned on me that more than just being about preparedness, this was a valuable lesson in doing more than what's expected of you. I was grateful for my job and even more grateful to have a manager willing to give me all the shifts I could handle. Moreover, I recognized my good fortune at working under someone who was willing to help me grow into a better employee.

When you know better, you do better—and if you're smart, you aim to do even more than that. There is no ceiling to your greatness, and it should be with that in mind that you take on every task, every role—every opportunity.

This moment may have been a small one in hindsight, but the magnitude of the lesson I learned that day is immeasurable. I was being gifted the opportunity to learn about being prepared. Where I might have thought I'd done everything expected of me, I was now being enlightened to the idea of expecting more from myself. Why should I be satisfied in doing the bare minimum? Why should an employer be satisfied in an employee who doesn't seek to rise above expectations? For me, it wasn't enough to just do my job—I needed to rise above the standards and set my own. This experience laid the early foundation for the work habits that I would go on to develop and continually strive to improve upon.

Weak work habits and a closed mind are not only damaging to you, but to everyone around you. It drives me crazy if someone on my team approaches his or her job with a poor attitude; it trickles down to every level and affects the team as a whole. Unfortunately, some people become complacent. They become so comfortable where they are, stagnant and unmoving, that they lose all desire to do more. It's that complacent attitude that can spread through a team very quickly. I've never understood why people would choose to stunt their own growth, but I give no excuses to those who do. Progress is a choice that we make by getting up every day with the mentality: "Here we go! I'm ready for anything! Let's do this!" It's a ripple effect to get up each day feeling self-motivated and aspiring to motivate those around you. Don't let your missteps derail you when their very purpose is to help get you on the right path. Enjoy what you do, stay the course and aim to beat your personal best every day.

We are only human, after all. Nobody's perfect. The greatest minds, the top achievers, have all gotten to where they are from a climb that was anything but strictly vertical.

Such people have paid their dues and made mistakes the likes of which have only worked to enhance the scale of their achievements. They've fallen, gotten back up and zigged and zagged their way to the top. If you were to ask them what stood out on their climb the most, you can bet it's those hard-earned lessons that packed the most punch. When I reflect on my life thus far, it's my mistakes that stand above the rest—those moments of trying to fit in and making poor decisions out of fear and doubt. It's having survived them and learned from them that has made all the difference.

Someone who knows all about learning and growing from experiences is Richard Branson, billionaire visionary and founder of the Virgin Group. An entrepreneur from the time he was in his early teens, Branson had his share of missteps throughout his career. Online via Virgin.com, under a blog post entitled *My Greatest Failure*, Branson cites such business failures as Virgin Cola and Virgin Brides as he credits his career to one rooted in countless mistakes—all of which led him to the successes that would then follow. It was a story from his early days as a young entrepreneur that really hit home for me, when Branson sought out to convince a major publishing house to buy one of his first business ventures, *Student Magazine*.

Branson explained that while the publishers wanted to focus in on things like distribution and other details, he was more interested in selling them on his ambitious plans for expanding the *Student* brand, growing from magazines to travel companies and even banks. Likely mistaking his enthusiasm for immaturity, the publishers quickly lost interest and Branson's pitch was a flop. Now, he credits this early "failure" as the catalyst that motivated him to further pursue those big dreams and businesses that he so strongly believed in.

What struck me most about his story was that, in this "failing," Branson might have seen the lesson as one in pulling back and being more "realistic" about his plans and ideas. Instead, he drew inspiration from their skepticism and pushed forward more determined than ever to see his dreams through. They couldn't see what he saw, but he remained focused, and he did it alone. I LOVE this story!

Your mistakes will undoubtedly help you in planning your next steps as you go, but that doesn't always mean that you were headed in the wrong direction to begin with. Sometimes, the lesson is about finding new angles and new approaches to getting what you want—even if your end goal remains unchanged.

More than just personal benefit, the ability to see your missteps in a positive light can also greatly impact the lives of others. From your experiences comes the opportunity to share what you know, to pay it all forward with your insight and advice. I count my mistakes as blessings for the fact that they've provided me with the kind of life experience others can truly benefit from. I'm able to impact the lives of those around me in a positive way by passing on what I've learned and helping others to understand the value in what they perceive only as their failings.

Every successful visionary knows the value in making mistakes. From rediscovering your purpose to fine-tuning your approach, every stumble will only help to get you into your stride. Have the foresight to approach your missteps with a positive outlook, and rework every miscalculation to your advantage. Again, it's all about translating your experiences into a language that helps you work toward your purpose. Get fluent in decoding your failings, and instead see them for the instrumental learning opportunities that they are to you. Always keep your purpose at the forefront of your mind, and engage an attitude that is geared towards a positive and open-minded perspective.

In 2015, I was asked to introduce Tony Robbins onto the stage at one of his motivational speaking seminars taking place in Toronto. A longtime fan, this was a major honour. I was so thrilled to have been asked that I hadn't considered just how intimidating a crowd of 5,000 people would be, or how warm those spotlights might feel from centre stage. It all became very real to me as I stood there in front of all of those expectant faces, thousands of captivated attendees ready-in-wait for the life-changing inspiration that Tony Robbins would no doubt deliver.

My children stood in the wings off stage. I looked back at them as I tried to calm my nerves, remembering what my eldest daughter had told me just moments before: "Just breathe slowly, Mom . . ."

This was supposed to be quick and easy, as I recalled my instructions to stick to the short script that had been supplied to me. The MC agreed that, when introducing me, he would join me in an impromptu dance onto the stage to engage and energize the crowd. "Happy" by Pharrell Williams had been my pick. I figured, even if my nerves took over and I lost my balance on my way to the podium, no one would notice if I was dancing!

A few lines into my introduction, I saw a small piece of paper flutter down on top of my pages. I looked down at the note, which read simply:

"SORRY! TONY'S NOT HERE, HE'S STUCK IN TRAFFIC!"

It had been the MC who'd slipped me the note. A standup comedian who was helping to host the event, he now stood beside me at the podium indicating to the note that only we could see. I looked over at him and whispered, trying to appear calm, "No surprise there, this is Toronto!"

Inside—my head was spinning. I wondered how I could be expected to keep this crowd engaged until the person they were *really* here to see showed up. I even fantasized about someone pulling the fire alarm to help get me off stage. What was I going to do? There was no "plan B" script in our notes . . .

I would just have to make it work! I forced a big smile toward the audience. Zoning in on the faces before me and meeting their eyes, I realized, these are really just *people*— and I know people. Sure, they weren't there to see me, but that didn't mean I didn't have some value to bring to the moment. I looked over at the MC and said, "Hey! Do you want to dance some more?" The crowd started laughing! I could work with this! Playing off the crowd, I kept the dialogue going between the MC and myself. The audience, obviously thinking all of this was planned, really got into it as we kept them laughing and engaged.

The MC began to ask me questions about my business, and I wondered what personal story I could tell that was appropriate for the moment. I felt my brain push forward memories of my own first Tony Robbins experience. I figured if ever there was a time and place for this story, it was then.

It was the early 90s and I was working out of one of my first brokerages as an agent. A road rep came into our office pitching a Tony Robbins event. At the time, Tony Robbins was a new and fresh voice in the motivational speaking circuit, and the business world was buzzing about his inspirational seminars and innovative methods. To say I was eager to go would have been an understatement, but tickets were expensive, and I just didn't have any funds to spare. At the time, things were tight enough as a single mother of three without spending on things that I couldn't really justify as necessities. Looking back, I laugh thinking about just how much of a "necessity" in my life that experience would actually turn out to be. Talk about hidden opportunities!

The rep was persistent. When I told him I just couldn't afford to go, he struck back with "Lady, you can't afford NOT to go!" WOW—he got me with that one! I was intrigued, and his insistence triggered something at my core. Something very powerful washed over me as I realized he was right. I just *felt* I couldn't afford to miss this. Somehow, I knew I needed it and that this was somewhere I needed to be. I had to make it work. I paid for the ticket with my credit card, knowing I would be making payments in installments until it could be covered in full. This would be worth every penny. I could feel it.

Before I knew it, the day of the event had come. By the time I'd dropped my kids off at school and rushed over, it was standing room only. At that point in time, there was none of the flash you might expect to see today: no big screens, no fancy lighting or celebrity cameos. There was just Tony himself, alone on stage, speaking to the crowd. And yet, that was more than enough.

I watched on as this man who seemed larger than life completely captivated a room packed full of people, his booming voice reverberating off the walls. I was so engrossed that it felt as though he was speaking directly to me. He told the story of how he used to live in a tiny apartment, overweight and depressed. He spoke about his early life and the steps he had taken to get himself out of a bad situation, experiences he felt could one day help someone else.

I was hanging on to his every word. Here was someone who was proof-positive of the power in living out your true purpose. I thought to myself, *If he can do it, if he can get himself out of a bad situation coming from where he came from, then I can too.* From that moment on, there was no turning back. I WAS GOING TO DO IT. Tony Robbins had reminded me that no matter what your situation, no matter how bad it got, there was always a way out. It all starts with you and your mindset.

That day was a game-changer for me, and it had everything to do with my perspective. After all, nothing had *really* changed as I walked out of that hall and back into my own world. There had been no magical turnover or sudden shift in my life. Yet, through my perspective, I started to see things in a new light. I was no longer that same person who had once found herself at such a low point, or that person who, having lost her home, her marriage and any sense of security, had been left feeling like a loser. I didn't have to feel that way anymore; I could choose to move forward.

Tony's words had further motivated me to begin translating the language of my life differently, opening myself up to the endless opportunities around me and getting over the sting of past mistakes by seeing them in a new light.

As my story ended, and my time on stage was nearly over, I reflected on one of the most pivotal moments of my career—when the opportunity of buying a brokerage came onto my path and I almost let fear take over. At the time, I had struggled to understand how this opportunity could be the right thing for me if it so greatly deviated from the plan I had in place. Grappling with doubt, I remembered Tony's words: "If it doesn't fit the plan, SO WHAT? CHANGE YOUR PLAN AND LAND ON YOUR FEET!"

As my extended time on stage came to a close—23 minutes to be exact—you could feel the energy from the crowd swell to the point that it was almost anticlimactic when the man of the hour showed up. Tony even hung back on stage for a moment to watch us in action! When I was finally given the go-ahead to introduce him, the crowd went wild. It was just before he did his signature run and jump onto the stage that he took a moment to say, "Great intro, Vivian."

Oh, my God! I remember thinking—did I just come face to face with TONY ROBBINS?!

My first experience at his show those years ago had helped to spark a new outlook on life for me—that, and the knowledge that I wasn't going to do it alone. After the brokerage agreement had been put into motion, I remember going home and holding a family meeting with my kids. The four of us sat around the table as I looked into their eyes and told them, "You are my team, I'm going to need you every step of the way." I wasn't trying to take over the world or become a titan of industry; I just wanted some security for my family, and some peace of mind for myself!

Admittedly, beyond the monumental need for the support of my children, I had ulterior motives—doesn't a mother always when it comes to the best interest of her kids? These were three teenagers, embarking on a phase of their life in which they would need direction and guidance the most. I wondered how these big changes, coupled with the divorce, would affect them during this critical time? Initially, the thought of buying the brokerage had me concerned about my children and the influence this new role would have on my ability to be as involved in their lives as I needed to be. If this was going to work, I would need to bring them in. I needed their support. It was the only way I would be able to maintain that connection with my three kids during this time of major change in our lives. It wasn't the easiest solution, as anyone who's ever brought their children to work knows full well, but with the bigger picture in mind, it was going to be okay—I would make it work.

So, I had my kids—my "team," really—on board with me from the ground up. My experience at that event and my understanding of how to go forward and use the lessons of past mistakes to my benefit had me feeling renewed and re-energized for whatever lay ahead. I was now able to decipher the limitless potential behind this new challenge and visualize just what an incredible journey it could be, not just for myself, but for my family as well.

My mind was set on the positive and my perspective was locked on the future. My mistakes and the lessons they had armed me with had brought me to this point, and from here I couldn't lose.

CHAPTER ELEVEN

AGAINST THE ODDS

The person who follows the crowd will usually go no further than the crowd. The person who walks alone is likely to find himself in places no one has ever seen before.
—Albert Einstein

When I think about *courage,* standing apart from the crowd, and the early markings of a leader, I go back to those lessons and stories I learned early on, from my earliest teachers; these lessons would stay with me for decades to come.

In 1969, when I was 14 years old, my parents took my brother and me to Italy to visit my grandparents over Christmas. To say I was excited would have been an understatement. I was young, and filled with endless expectations for what it would be like to visit Italy, the place my family had come from, the one we had left behind for the life we'd made here. Before leaving, I told my teachers and friends in excitement. They were so excited for me, and my teacher suggested I keep a journal to share with everyone upon my return. It wasn't lost on me that, for ten years before this, we'd watched as our father would pack a bag and leave for

Italy over Christmas, leaving one family to visit the one he'd left behind. *Finally, it was my turn to go as well!*

I couldn't harness my excitement as I dreamed about what it would be like once we landed in Rome! Having watched *Gidget Goes to Rome*, a reel of anticipation ran through my mind: the Trevi Fountain, the shops, the fashion . . . I couldn't wait. *I was Gidget!*

Our flight touched down in the dead of winter. We then headed toward my grandparents' home, situated one hour south of Rome. At this point, our plans had already shifted, due to some unforeseen circumstances. As soon as we had landed, we'd gotten the news that my grandfather on my mother's side had fallen ill with influenza. My parents decided it would be best to go to my grandparents' farm first, before heading to the hospital where my mothers' father was the following day.

As the bright lights and impressive architecture of the city of Rome started to peel away, the picturesque landscape became highways—vast and empty. Those highways then became winding roads that grew narrower as we headed up hill after hill to our destination. I could see the dirt trails on either side of the road, blocked in with uneven walls of stacked stone. When we finally pulled up to a run-down farmhouse, I felt my heart sink. This was going to be home for the next three weeks?! It was far from anything I had expected. I was in the middle of nowhere.

Determined not to say anything that might make me seem ungrateful, I said very little. On the inside, however, I felt my high hopes for the trip come crashing down before me as I stood, staring at a scene that looked like something out of an Alfred Hitchcock movie. This was not at all what I had expected. Until that moment, I had never considered myself a pampered kid, but I was in for a rude awakening.

The first shock to my system was the water situation. By that I mean there was no running water. There was also no formal bathroom; and by "formal," I mean there was *no bathroom!* Quite simply, if you had to go, you took your business out back. Call me a lover of luxury, but I had become somewhat accustomed to the idea of a toilet, sink, four walls and a door. Add to that the fact there was no phone or TV, and I wondered what I was supposed to do to pass the time. Knowing my parents would be leaving soon to be with my mother's family, I felt the fear of the unknown wash over me. It was as though there was a sense of abandonment looming overhead, as I knew it would soon just be me and my younger brother left here, in this strange place, with two elderly people I barely knew.

The next day, my parents took their leave for the hospital. The prognosis didn't look good for my grandfather, and my mother was eager to be by his side. As I watched my parents pull out onto the road and drive away, I don't think I blinked once as their taillights vanished in the distance. I swallowed hard and put on a brave face, but I felt completely abandoned. *Help!* I felt myself screaming after them silently, *Don't leave me here! I'm scared, and I don't even have TV!*

My mother's father passed away that same week. What was meant to be a family trip quickly became just my brother and I left to our own devices in my grandparents' farmhouse. My parents had spent the first few days of our trip at the hospital and now made their way to be with my mother's family to help with funeral arrangements.

So here I was, 14 years old, feeling out of place in a house that terrified me with its blank walls, concrete floors and drafty doorways. Apparently, I had been born in this house, and yet everything about it felt cold and unfamiliar. I'd been left to look after my little brother with only my grandparents for company: two people I barely felt I knew, and whose home had none of the basic luxuries I had become accustomed to. This was a massive shock to my system, to say the least. Luckily, a ray of hope formed when I discovered an old transistor radio in the house one day. I started turning the knobs, and it worked! Finally armed with some connection to the outside world, I took the radio up to the room I was staying in and entertained myself there for hours.

As far as the bathroom situation went, my grandfather, who sensed my horror at the limited options, decided to make me my very own "private bathroom" outside. It wasn't more than a hole in the ground, but he did his best to provide me with some privacy by stacking up branches around the small ditch. He even offered me an umbrella when an onset of evening rain made the whole thing hysterical. From his kindness and concern for my comfort, I fell in love with my grandfather—this elderly man who had initially felt like such a stranger to me.

Needless to say, it was an early lesson for me in adapting to your situations and finding humour in your circumstances. It became one of those "laugh or cry" situations; where, after some crying, I ultimately chose to laugh. If I'd ever felt justified in complaining about the things we didn't have back home, that sentiment was long gone.

Once the initial shock of my surroundings faded, I began to take in everything around me. I found comfort in hearing the roosters in the morning, watching my grandparents go about their daily activities, checking in on the chickens pecking away at their food. I would play with the stray puppy that would come running onto the grounds. These things sparked some simple joy for me, giving me some sense of normalcy, as I realized, *There really is life out here!*

It was around this time that I finally got around to getting to know my grandparents. My grandmother, I discovered, cried a lot. It seemed to me to be a mix of joy and sadness. She started crying the day we arrived and continued crying in anticipation of the day we would have to leave. It was abundantly clear to me just how much she missed having my father around. My grandfather, however, showed less emotion outright. His and my grandmother's routines became a sort of comfort in their consistency for me during our stay. Each day at the crack of dawn, my grandparents would get up and make their way down the stairs and into the kitchen. I would watch as my grandfather, this strong and solid man, would sit by the fire, hunched over in a wooden chair just big enough to fit his frame. His movements, down to the smallest gesture, were slow and methodical as he would put his pipe to the flame and lean towards the small fire, stoking it, as his pot of fresh beans would begin to cook. All the while, my grandmother busied herself around him. The two of them were like ships in the night as they went about their routines, in their simple, quiet life. My grandfather's days were set in an almost militant fashion: always awake at dawn, and never up past 6:30pm.

I was nearly a week into my stay, and eating little of the food that seemed so foreign to me, I was already shedding the first of the fifteen pounds that I would lose during the trip. I was basically living on tangerines! On one of these early mornings, with the weather outside damp and cold, I pulled up a small stool next to my grandfather. He sat, with his pipe hanging out the side of his mouth, lurched forward and prodding at his beans in the fire. I remember vividly the moment when, keeping his eyes on the flames, he suddenly began speaking to me in English. I nearly fell off my stool!

"Nonno, how do you know how to speak English?!" I asked him.

Never peeling his gaze from the fire, he started on, in good English, about his early life. He began to tell me how, in his 20s (he was well into his 80s by this time) he had worked out of train stations in Chicago, New York and Pennsylvania. His job had been to announce the trains as they pulled in. He'd even spent some time in England, doing the same kind of work. All in all, he'd spent nearly fifteen years abroad before returning home, he told me. I sat there, my mouth gaping wide. In a mix of shock and confusion, I cautiously asked him the only thing that came to mind, mindful of the fact that he might take offense to it.

"But, Nonno . . . why did you come back?"

I just couldn't understand why this man had travelled so far at such a young age, found steady work and paid his dues, even picked up on the language—only to return. And to return to what? This place must have been such a far cry from the bright lights, big cities and abundance of culture he had seen. Why would anyone make the effort to leave, only to come back to this?

I remember the ash falling from his pipe as he leaned back from where he sat, his eyes still glued on the flames in front of him. The heat and smoke made my eyes water, but he seemed immune. He paused for such a while I thought maybe he hadn't heard me, and just as I opened my mouth to repeat the question, he spoke.

"I was afraid."

Afraid? Had I heard wrong? Is it possible he thought that word meant something else in English? Surely, he didn't mean *afraid*. Here was this tall, intimidating man—and this was in his old age. In his younger days, I can't imagine him as having reason to be scared of anything! Surely this man, who stood at over 6 feet tall, with bear hands that now gently poked at the beans before him wasn't telling me he had left it all behind out of *fear*.

He explained that he had feared what *could* happen. It was during his time working at the train station in Chicago that he began to feel the pace of the world around him shift more quickly that he'd ever expected. He suddenly found himself faced with the unknown, and he feared what could happen and what might lie ahead if he stuck it out. He was afraid of change.

My limited life experience at the time made it difficult for me to consider factors other than fear that might have drawn my grandfather back home. In retrospect, I now see that beyond his fear of the unknown, there might have been other elements at play; emotional ties that called him back maybe, ones that wouldn't be so hard to relate to now. I felt sadness for him in that moment. Who knows what he might have seen, what he might have accomplished, or how his life might have been if he hadn't returned?

I will never forget that day. I still remember what my grandfather looked like as he sat there and stared into that fire. Later in life, I would often flash back to that moment and wonder what it was he was seeing beyond those flames. What had he held on to from that time of his life? With so many years behind him, settled into a life that was so simple and certain, he'd still held onto the language of a place he would never return to, a life he would never know. I couldn't help but wonder—did he feel regret for the life he left behind, or what could have been?

It still baffles me, when I think back on this memory and on this time in my life. I was just fourteen, so inexperienced with the world, such a novice to everything around me. Still, I couldn't imagine a fear so strong that it would have me give up on the possibility of a life so different than that one on the farm. I think about the pressures my grandfather must have faced, the scrutiny of leaving home right around the time when his family would have looked to him the most, expecting him to live up to his responsibilities as a son. The courage to leave could only have been matched by his desire for something different than what lay before him. Yet, when push came to shove, his fear of the unknown drew him back. That's the part that puzzled me, that's the part I could never forget.

When I think about "going against the odds," the concept of courage and the notion of sacrifice come to mind. For those of us who are not first generation—those of us who are the children or grandchildren of family that came before—our relatives made the ultimate sacrifice. They left everything they knew to start a life that might offer the next generations the kind of opportunities they could only dream of. I make the connection between this and my own journey—my desire to lead, my aspirations that lay beyond the beaten path. I was looking for the kind of stability for my family and myself that could only be crafted by my own hand. At every step of the way, I had to stick my neck out and take some kind of risk, never guaranteed of the outcome. Fear was always there to try and deter me, but giving in to it was never an option. Something within me just always seemed hell bent on doing more, going further, making it work—just doing it.

When I was just three years old, my parents made the decision to uproot our young family and move to Canada. Whenever I think of my grandfather, I think of my father, and the parallels they shared in their early lives. Both men left behind everything they'd known and made their way to a place that was completely foreign to them and held no promises or guarantees. The difference was that my father didn't make this trip alone; he took with him an entire family. I can't imagine the pressures he faced.

My parents both sacrificed everything in the hopes of securing a future for us that held more opportunity than the one we might have had if we'd stayed in Italy. I think of the guilt my father must have felt as he left behind his parents, breaking from the plans that had been set for him, defying the expectations of an only son. I consider the risk he and my mother took in uprooting their family and moving as immigrants to a place where neither the people nor the language would hold any familiarity to them. I wonder how they felt as they tried to make a home for the four of us out of a small, three-bedroom bungalow? Doing their best to keep us afloat, my mother worked at a cleaner's pressing shirts, while my father worked two jobs. More than anything else, I reflect on their sacrifice, day in and day out, as they worked tirelessly against every barrier to lay a foundation for us in this new world.

My parents could have let the fear of the unknown prevent them from making these sacrifices for their family, but instead they plowed forward, determined to create a new life for us. They immersed me and my siblings in our new surroundings and dedicated their lives to securing our futures. The hardships and ridicule they faced as immigrants were all for the benefit of what they viewed as the greater good—the potential for a better future for their family.

Now, when I think back to this, I think of the moment when the rug was pulled out from under me, and I was faced with the prospect of losing not only my job, but also the only livelihood I knew. All I could think about at that time was survival. I was fueled by my determination never to find myself vulnerable in that way again. I needed to not only persevere, but also prevent this from happening in the future. If I was going down, it would be on me, no one else. From there I came to the conclusion that I would have to be the one to create security for my life, despite all the doubt and fear that would come with that. After all, I had no knowledge of professional accounting, no clue how to read financial statements—not the slightest understanding of what it meant to be "in the black" or "red"—and yet, if I bought the office, I would be responsible for things like payroll, rent, taxes, employees—how would I manage?

Here is where the odds truly felt stacked against me. It was survival, and I felt at a disadvantage. I needed to somehow rise above all of that and do what needed to be done. I needed to secure my future, and if that meant buying my job, so be it. Even racked with stress at the uncertainty that lay ahead, I reflected on my beginnings. I thought of what my parents suffered through so that I might one day be fortunate enough to find myself here, surrounded by opportunities. I was able to minimize the fear I felt by drawing parallels to what my parents had done for their family, for us. After all, it wasn't as though I had to cross an ocean, I just had to put one foot in front of the other and head out into the fog. The memories of my parents' struggle and sacrifice and the image of my grandfather staring into the fire all pushed me to refocus and work through what I needed to, in spite of my uncertainties.

My parents had given me an early lesson in sacrifice and had equipped me with the strength to persevere by their example. From there, it was up to me to ensure their efforts hadn't been in vain. I mean, *at least we had running water!* If I could manage with a hole in the ground and no phone or television, I could handle this too!

Retreating was not an option, so I rationalized with myself and broke it all down. I came back to the idea of team building, finding where my strengths would lie in this new role, and bringing the right people on board. In these moments where you feel lost in the fog, it's all about getting your mind working, and finding a way to refocus. Putting one foot in front of the other. If it helps, write things down, put some Post-It notes up on your mirror, whatever it takes to break it all down. This will make it more manageable for you, because truly, everything is manageable—even if it doesn't feel that way at the start.

I'll be the first to admit, in the most overwhelming moments of it all, I wanted to scream, yell, and cry out for help! But none of that would have helped me. What did help was pulling back from the anxiety I felt and slowing my mind down to where I could reason, *Ok, Vivian, one thing at a time. You can't let the fear get to you. Break it down. Prioritize. One day at a time. One step at a time.* That's really all it takes to get started. Don't let barriers keep you from your goals. You need to move past them and embrace who you are early on; forgiving yourself for the stumbles you make along the way. You have to continue moving forward, pushing through whatever comes your way. Stop beating yourself up and allow the whole you to emerge, the *real* you—you know who I'm talking about! Get re-acquainted with that person!

Though I spent a lot of time trying to fit the mold—inside, I always knew I was different. I've run towards the unknown and gone against the grain for as long as I can remember, often while riddled with guilt because all I wanted to do was fit in. It hasn't always been easy, and it's almost never been a comfortable experience—but it's been my own. My journey has been, and will continue to be, one I pave for myself, no beaten path required. Forget the blueprint—you just don't need it. Make your own way and build your own happiness, whatever that looks like for you.

I wish for you the clarity of mind to appreciate everything God has given you, the good, the bad, all of it! I want you to take your past experiences and use them to pave the path toward your ultimate life. It's yours to live, and don't let anyone tell you differently! Learn to FORGIVE yourself and unleash the WHOLE you. Tap into that immeasurable power within and have faith that you are your own greatest ally—because you are. Don't let anyone or anything stop you from being the person you were meant to be.

FINAL THOUGHTS

So here we are at the end of this book, and just like the beginning, I find myself grappling with how to turn my thoughts into words. It feels almost impossible for me to fully express just how grateful I am for the support of my family throughout this process. In particular, my children Michelle, Julie and Justin, who along with all my grandchildren—Alexandra, Jonathan, Elias, Victoria, Sofia and Matthew—are in my first thoughts when I wake up in the morning and my final thoughts at night. This book would not have been possible without the love and support of my parents, whose influence and guidance have impacted me at countless points in my journey, along with my siblings. It goes without saying, sincerest gratitude to my agents, who inspire me to go into work every day and have certainly put their stamp on these pages.

This adventure, like so many in my life, was completely unexpected—and more worthwhile for having caught me off guard. From the beginning of this project, my aim has been to use my experiences and personal philosophies to add some value to the lives of those who read these pages and share in my journey.

Admittedly, at the start, I was unsure about what I wanted to share. I had a hard time deciding which of my life experiences might make the most impact in the lives of others. How do you comb through a lifetime of lessons and select only a few—where would I even start? But then I decided that my focus shouldn't be on what you might take, but rather, on what I could *give*. From there, the lessons and personal stories, it all seemed to flow organically; and that's when I realized, though I'd never planned on writing a book, my stories had already begun to write themselves.

Ultimately, in putting these pages together, I came to see just how interconnected the lessons of my life have been, and that they have always, in one way or another, centered on the passage toward my purpose.

If there's one philosophy I hope will stick with you from these pages, it's that of finding your own purpose. When you know what it is that drives you, the world will open up to you. It really is an incredible feeling to wake up each day and know that you are doing exactly what it is you're meant to do. It doesn't matter at what point in your life you arrive at this discovery, only that you recognize it and take action when you do.

It's a funny thing to sit down and relive the most impactful moments of your life. Suddenly, as you revisit old memories and feel the spark of familiar lessons come to surface, you're reminded of just how far you've come. I look around, and I feel a sense of pride—not only for my family and myself; but also, for the people around me who are making great strides each day on their own journeys. There is no greater satisfaction than the knowledge that your life's stepping-stones have somehow positively influenced the steps of others.

No one's path toward his or her own authentic life is an easy one. It's never simply a one-way climb, and I hope you know you aren't alone in stumbling along the way. What I wish for you is the strength of mind to know you are absolutely capable of seeing the journey through. You have everything you need to make your way in this world—it's all there within you! But it's up to you to get started; only YOU can take those first steps from wherever it is you find yourself now. Once you decide your life is worth living authentically, and with your greatest purpose in mind—you will be unstoppable!

We all have this one life, with no guarantees of time, and certainly no promise of a second try—so make it count! Make every moment worthwhile. See every obstacle as an opportunity and never let it slow you down. Be ferocious in your determination to see through to your goals, always with the mentality that giving up is not an option.

My life changed for the better when I decided that it should. It was intentional, difficult and exhausting—and the most rewarding shift in perspective I've ever made. Suddenly every struggle seemed worth it because I was focused on my purpose, and my biggest motivation—my children—was set clear as crystal in my mind. I knew what was at stake, and that was all I needed. I hope for you the ability to see your best life as one worth fighting for, and to know you are worth every ounce of effort. Because you ARE worth it—and you can do ANYTHING.

So, what are you waiting for? Find your motivation and let it move you!

Get beyond the limits set for you—get beyond the fear—get past all of it. Sync up with your own inner philosophy and pay close attention to those instincts as you make your way into the future. Let the fear and uncertainty motivate you. Be a visionary and dare to be different. Do more than expected—be unique in your ambitions and set the bar high!

Never be afraid to be who you are. Your strengths are in the things that set you apart. That's what makes you unique and capable of wonderful things. Never deny yourself the opportunity to go after them. Be proactive in your own life story. It has to start with you. Believe in yourself and never lose focus. Everything you want is within reach, you just have to keep at it!

COMMIT to the goal of living an authentic life. Don't succumb to the pressures of others and never mold your life around their expectations. Do what you need to do as many times as it takes to see it through. Embrace all your experiences because they all brought you right here, to this moment.

This is your sign. This is your moment. Take it.

Do everything in your power to live out your purpose, because in the story of your life—it all begins and ends with YOU!